DON QUIXOTE

AN INTRODUCTORY ESSAY
IN PSYCHOLOGY

DON QUIXOTE

AN INTRODUCTORY ESSAY
IN PSYCHOLOGY

SALVADOR DE MADARIAGA

London
OXFORD UNIVERSITY PRESS

Oxford University Press, Ely House, London W.1

GLASGOW NEW YORK TORONTO MELBOURNE WELLINGTON
CAPE TOWN SALISBURY IBADAN NAIROBI LUSAKA ADDIS ABABA
BOMBAY CALCUTTA MADRAS KARACHI LAHORE DACCA
KUALA LUMPUR HONG KONG

First published (in a limited edition) by the Gregynog Press 1934
First published by the Oxford University Press 1935
Second Impression 1948
Revised Edition (with additional chapter) issued in OXFORD PAPERBACKS *1961*
Reprinted 1966

Printed in Great Britain by
Fletcher & Son Ltd, Norwich

Contents

Introduction

In the Life of Cervantes which Lockhart appended to his edition of Motteux's translation, I find the following words:

> In our country, almost everything that any sensible man would wish to hear said about *Don Quixote* has been said over and over again by writers whose sentiments I should be sorry to repeat without their words, and whose words I should scarcely be pardoned for repeating.

There is hardly a work—whether of criticism or of imagination—which has not at its inception to surmount this paralysing thought. Yet, works do get written—fortunately for the most part—a sign that the argument put forward by Lockhart, whatever its merits as an argument, has little power in the realm of the will. Needless to say, even as an argument, it is fallacious, for it rests on the assumption that a work of art, such as *Don Quixote*, is a static thing, a block of matter, be this matter words, marble, or colour-pastes, which once put into shape remains for ever what it was when it left the hands of the artist. This view, however, misses the main features, nay, the very essence of a work of art, which is not merely matter and shape, but matter formed by the spirit. The specific character of a work of art, that which separates it not merely from formless matter but from works achieved without inspiration, is that it *lives*. It is conceived and created, and long after its creator has shed his mortal garment, it continues to grow. For us, children of the twentieth century, *Westminster Abbey*, *Hamlet*, Beethoven's *Ninth Symphony*, Michael Angelo's *Moses*, are not what they were for the coevals of their respective creators, for they have since then assimilated centuries of mankind's spiritual growth. That is why, despite Lockhart's discouraging advice, we may venture to speak of *Don Quixote*, for though our own wits be poorer than those of the critics of yesteryear, Don Quixote is greater than when, armed cap-à-pie, he came out of Cervantes' imagination—greater for all the wealth of experience and adventure which he has gone through while riding for three hundred years over the boundless fields of the human spirit.

For think of the road which the spirit of the Brave Knight has covered since, towards the beginning of the seventeenth century, he died in the flesh, unable to bear the melancholy burden of sanity. Luscinda no longer looks for Cardenio's letters in his copy of *Amadís de Gaul*, but talks to him freely in the stalls at the 'Pictures' while justifying Boileau's wise remark:

Chassez le naturel, il revient au gallop.

Amadís himself, whom Cervantes thought he had chased for ever, gallops back on the screen, clad in cow-boy's attire, and achieves feats no less extravagant than those which turned the brain of poor *Quixano el Bueno*. Arms and letters, the two professions which then governed the world, and which Don Quixote, as an expert in both, loved to compare and contrast, have fallen to the second rank; while the 'fatal words *thine* and *mine*' which the Brave Knight stigmatized in his speech to the goatherds have become the α and ω of the science of government, and those very windmills and fulling mills which he fought, or meant to fight, have grown to be what his wild imagination fancied and seems to have guessed—giants of industry whose hundred powerful arms encircle the world, awe-inspiring powers which work in the night. Sancho's ambition to become the governor of an island has since then entered the hearts of the innumerable Sanchos who people the earth, so that, as there were not enough islands to satisfy so many would-be governors, and as, moreover, no natives were left to be governed, since even Sancho's Baratarian subjects had come to emulate the ambition of their lord, the matter had to be entrusted to enchanters. A famous magician, by the name of Rousseau, succeeded in enchanting the Island Barataria in such a manner that all became at the same time governors and governed—and he confirmed this enchanted commonwealth with the fantastic name of Democracy. The which name, if Don Quixote in his scholarship would recognize it as meaning 'the power of the people', Sancho in his simpler common sense would certainly hold demoniacal and understand as 'the power of the devil'.

And thus, over earth and mind, three centuries of experience have passed, during which many an illusory castle has turned out to be an inn; many a beautiful Dulcinea has been enchanted into a rough and ill-smelling country wench. Religious unity in Europe, the American Eldorado, the dreams of the Age of Reason, the windmills of the Bastille, dream after dream and adventure after adventure—the ghost of Don Quixote has gone through since they laid his body to rest. Can we speak of him as did his contemporaries who saw him ride the plains of La Mancha?

Can we even speak of him as did Cervantes? There

is a pregnant line in Cervantes' own preface to his great book :

But I, who though seeming to be the father, am the step-father of Don Quixote . . .

A line which deserves to be weighed and meditated. A line in which Cervantes with that intuition which is the crowning gift of creative genius seems to realize that Don Quixote is really Nature's son and not his own, and to guess that this 'dry, swarthy son', *hijo seco y avellanado*, will grow in the course of ages to reach a greatness far beyond the dreams of his stepfather.

There is little doubt that Cervantes ill-treats Don Quixote now and then with the hard hand of a conventional stepfather. True at the very root of his story lies the right of sanity to correct madness by means of ridicule—for indeed it seems as if Cervantes had anticipated Bergson's theory of laughter as the social policeman set against the vagaries of the individual. Yet, with Cervantes, we feel that this policeman is now and then a bit of a bully. Having created in Don Quixote so noble a type, Cervantes might have seen that we should resent the infliction of unnecessary hardship upon him. When his own folly exposes him to ridicule we are ready to laugh remorselessly. When he is wantonly made ridiculous we are sorry for him and laughter fails. Such scenes are not entirely lacking in the story. Thus Don Quixote's arrival before the Duke and Duchess : Part II, Chapter xxx :

And now Don Quixote drew nigh with his vizor up; and Sancho, seeing him offer to alight, hastened to hold his stirrup; but as ill-luck would have it, as he was getting off Rucio, he entangled his foot in one of the ropes of the pack-saddle, so that not being able to get it out, he hung by the heel, with his mouth and breast to the ground. Don Quixote, who was used to have his stirrup held when he dismounted, thinking Sancho had hold of it already, came suddenly with the weight of his body upon it, bringing down with himself Rocinante's saddle which must have been ill-girt, and saddle and knight came to the ground not without much confusion on his part and many a muttered curse against Sancho, who was all the while with his foot in the stocks.

There is no point whatever in this humiliation of Don Quixote. The scene is not inevitable, it is therefore unnecessary—and, like all unnecessary evil, it is painful to the mind. For Cervantes, Don Quixote is too often a mere object for merry-making. He criticizes the Duke and the Duchess for the trouble they took in making fun of Don Quixote and Sancho:

And Cide Hamete adds that he holds the mockers to be as mad as the mocked, and that the Duke and Duchess were within two fingers' breadth of passing as fools since they took so much trouble to make fun of two who were so. (Part II, Chapter xxx.)

Yet here it is the excess rather than the thing itself which Cervantes is attacking—while in many a passage he shows his whole-hearted sympathy with the merry-makers. Such an approval is implied in the following sentence:

Dorothea, who was discreet and very witty, knowing the little sense of Don Quixote and that all save Sancho made fun of him . . . (Part I, Chapter xxx.)

True, the author is an elusive personality, no less complex than his creation. There is a sentence—one of those passing sentences of Cervantes which sometimes mean so much—in which he aptly expresses that feeling of reluctant and unwelcome merriment which some of the Brave Knight's adventures inspire in us.

Now, gentle reader, let Sancho depart in peace and god-speed, and look forward to whole bushels of laughter which the story of his government will cause you; and meanwhile, listen to what befell his master the same night; though it do not make you laugh outright, it may at least make you draw back your lips, with monkey laughter, for Don Quixote's adventures must be celebrated either with laughter or with wonderment. (Part II, Chapter xliv.)

In these last words we would fain see a warning against a possible misunderstanding of Cervantes' attitude towards his own hero. Cervantes realizes that laughter cannot be whole-hearted when raised at the expense of a noble character, since man's deepest instinct leads him to recognize his own ideal self in all that is noble and when we laugh at our own selves we can only laugh with 'monkey laughter'. Often, however, Cervantes seems to forget this mood and join the crowd of merry-makers. At times, we wish that he had not submitted his hero to certain indignities which the flesh is heir to. And there is even one page which every reader of *Don Quixote* would wish unwritten. While Sancho sleeps, Don Quixote has been brooding over his servant's remissness in not lashing himself in order to disenchant Dulcinea.

Full of that conceit, he came up to Sancho, having first taken the reins of Rocinante, and fitted them so as to be able to lash Sancho with them. He then began to undo Sancho's breech-sashes (though it is said that he had but the front one) but he had no sooner come to him than

Sancho started up thoroughly awake, and said: 'What is that? Who is there touching me and untrussing me?' 'It is I,' answered Don Quixote, 'coming to repair thy negligence and to alleviate my torment: I am come to whip thee, Sancho, and to discharge in part that debt for which thou standst engaged. Dulcinea perishes, thou livest careless and I die with longing; strip therefore, of thy own will, for it is my will in this solitary spot, to give thee at least two thousand lashes.' 'None of that,' said Sancho. 'Let your Worship be quiet, for if not, Heaven knows deaf men shall hear us. The lashes I am bound to are to be voluntary, not by force, and just now I have no mind to whip myself. Let your Worship be content with my promise that I will flog and fly-lap myself when the humour takes me.' 'There is no leaving it to your courtesy, Sancho,' said Don Quixote, 'for thou art hard-hearted; and though a churl, thou art tender of flesh.' And forthwith he tried and strove to strip him. Seeing which, Sancho started up on his feet, and falling upon his master, wrestled with him, tripped up his heels, and threw him down upon his back; then he set his knee upon his master's breast and held his hands in his own so that he did neither let him roll over nor breathe. Don Quixote said to him: 'How now, traitor? Rebel against thy master and natural lord? Stand up against him that gives thee his bread?' 'King I neither make nor mar,' answered Sancho, 'but help myself who am my lord. Let your Worship promise to keep quiet and not to whip me now, and I will let your Worship go free and at liberty: if not,

> "Here thou diest, traitor,
> Foe to Dona Sancha".'

Don Quixote gave his word and swore by the life of his thoughts not to touch a hair of his raiment, but entirely leave it to his will and discretion to whip himself when he thought fit. (Part II, Chapter lx.)

This passage, hard enough in its substance, is rendered harder by the somewhat perfunctory manner in which it is written, and the reader is pained to find that, after an event of so deep a significance, Cervantes can pass on to the next adventure, without the slightest development or comment. The incident, it is true, occurs in that part of the book in which Cervantes is working against time to counter the effect produced by the publication of the spurious second part. Yet, it is too much in harmony with that curious animosity against Don Quixote, which now and then seems to harden Cervantes' pen, to be lightly dismissed as the result of hurried composition.

But again, Cervantes did not and could not see Don Quixote in his true greatness—which, so far as we are concerned, is the greatness that he has attained today. Numberless—and futile—discussions have been wasted on the question whether Cervantes meant to give his characters the symbolic value which we now attach to them. The quarrel is based on a misunderstanding of the very essence of art, of true, that is, creative art, which is concerned purely with creation in the concrete, but which, when successful, attains a symbolic value by the very fact that it is creative. This virtue does not reside in genius but in nature. It is the outcome of the universal unity and harmony of things. Had Cervantes meant to symbolize abstractions, he would have failed to create a work of art. He was, however, purely concerned with creating characters, and that is why he succeeded in giving the world eternal symbols. For even as a stone that strikes the water, though merely intent on obeying the law of gravity, will cause ever-widening circles to rise on the surface of the liquid, even so the creator that succeeds in touching the sea of the spirit will stir circles on it beyond the bounds of his limited sight. Not what Cervantes meant, but what he did is our patrimony, and when speaking of *Don Quixote* we can choose any of the infinite number of circles which surge wider and wider round the spot where the book first fell.

Cervantes and his Time

BORN in October, 1547, Cervantes begins life when the power and glory of Spain are at their highest. In 1492 Ferdinand and Isabel had conquered Granada and brought under the same Crown all the Peninsular Kingdoms but Portugal. In the same year, 1492, Columbus had discovered America. In 1517, Charles, their grandson, born and bred in Flanders, had begun to rule Spain. In 1519 he had been elected Emperor of Germany. In 1521 while he was away in Germany his troops had defeated at Villalar the rebel Commoners who stood for Spanish parliamentary freedom against the absolute ways of the Flemish King. In 1522 Charles V had returned to Spain with an army of 4,000 Germans and a swarm of Flemish hangers-on who, despite Spanish advice, had incited the King Emperor to a ruthless repression of the Commoners. Thus, by the way, did the Low Countries sow in Spain the seeds of their own oppression in the following reign.

But the loss of freedom had been drowned in the light of further wonders. In 1519–26, with 315 Spaniards, 7 cannon, and 16 horse, Cortés had conquered Mexico. During the same two years, 1519–21, Magellan had discovered the Straits, and the Philippine Islands; and his lieutenant, Elcano, had circumnavigated the world for the first time; in 1525, Charles' troops had defeated Francis I at Pavia, and the most brilliant of the Kings of France had had to spend a year in Madrid as a prisoner of war. In 1534, Pizarro had conquered Peru with 227 men; and Mendoza had founded Buenos Aires. In 1547, the very year of Cervantes' birth, Francis I, the stubborn enemy of Charles, had died and the Emperor had defeated the Protestant League at Mühlberg.

Cervantes was therefore born six months after the death of Francis I, about one year after the publication of the Third Book of Pantagruel, six years before the death of Rabelais. When Cervantes was nine and Montaigne twenty-three, the Great Emperor had abdicated before an astounded Christendom. It was therefore about this time, when the arch of Rabelais' life touches the earth and the arches of the lives of Montaigne and Cervantes rise in the sky, that the two great crowned knights leave the stage of European history which their rivalry had transfigured into a Romance of Chivalry. On January 22nd, 1528, at Burgos, Guienne, king at arms of Francis I, and Clarenceux, king at arms of Henry VIII, presented challenges to Charles on behalf of their respective masters. Charles reminded the King of France that, under the fourth clause of the Treaty of Madrid, Francis I was bound to return to captivity in Spain, since he had not fulfilled the terms of the Treaty within the delays ascribed in it; and that, should King Francis default, Charles V held the right to say that the King of France had behaved 'lâchement et méchamment'. Better still, on Easter Monday 1536, eleven years before the birth of Cervantes, when Montaigne was three and Rabelais forty-six, Charles V denounced his rival's policy before the Pope in a speech which ended in this singular way :

Therefore, I promise your Holiness, in the presence of this sacred college and of all these knights here present, if the King of France wishes to meet me in arms, man to man, I promise to meet him armed or unarmed, in my shirt, with sword and dagger, on land or sea, on a bridge or an island, in a closed field, or in front of our armies or wherever and however he may wish and it be fair.

It is difficult for us to realize the cumulative effect of all these events, some of which bordered on the unbelievable. The threat of the Reformation had come to add a kind of religious fervour to the mood of pride and self-confidence so many successes in both worlds had fostered in the Spaniards. Charles, who at seventeen had arrived in Spain as a Fleming, knowing no Spanish, had become a Spaniard at heart and would speak no other language at ceremonial and State occasions, though his mother tongue was French. His decision at last to stand against the Protestants—for fear lest the Reformation spread to his Low Countries —had invested him in the eyes of Spaniards with a kind of dignity as the First Crusader of Christendom. Nor did the Spaniards hold the Pope himself in greater awe, since His Holiness would indulge in power politics and all too often join forces with the King of France who was the ally of Turks and Protestants. In 1527, the year Philip II was born, an army of Spaniards and Germans, gathered together by Charles under the command of a French runagate, the Duke of Bourbon, and a German anti-papist, Frundsberg, broke loose—being in arrears of pay—and sacked Rome in dastardly fashion.

In 1547, the year of Cervantes' birth, the Council of the Church, so insistently demanded by the Emperor to reform the Church from within, sat at Trent and was brilliantly led by Spanish theologians. One year later, Charles sent to the Pope his ambassador, Don Diego de Mendoza ('great Aristotelian, mathematician, Greek and Latin scholar', one of the most assiduous collectors of Greek manuscripts then known), to protest against the transfer of the Council from Trent to Bologna. Don Diego was no man to mince matters. He knelt before the Pope, but spoke out with an imperial voice. The Pope, with a treaty with France in his pocket, asked the Ambassador to bear in mind that he was not in his house; whereupon, Don Diego retorted : 'I am a knight, and so was my father. As such, I must carry out my lord's command to the letter, without any fear of His Holiness, though with due reverence for the Vicar of Christ; and, since I am a Minister of the Emperor, I am in my house wherever I set foot.' These words pronounced in the colourful setting of a solemn Papal Consistory, are typical in more ways than one of the age in which Cervantes was born. They convey the self assurance the great servants of the Emperor then felt as men who were at home in the whole world, since the whole world was the house and territory of the Imperial Sovereignty; and they reveal to what an extent that world, already modern, was still rooted in the mediaeval conception of knighthood.

'I am a Knight, and so was my father'—proudly asserts Don Diego de Mendoza. The child was one year old then who, at the close of that century was to write the greatest novel ever written on the grandeur and misery of knighthood.

2

He was born in Alcalá de Henares then one of the centres of learning in Christendom. In this little city close to Madrid, Cisneros, known in English speaking lands by his first name of Cardinal Ximenez, had founded in 1508 a university specially devoted to the languages of antiquity. He had collected there the best humanists and philologists he could find, including a Greek and several Jews, and had financed that monument of learning the Polyglot Bible, printed in Hebrew, Greek, Chaldean, and Latin and published in 1520. Alcalá had been the centre of Erasmism in Spain; and both the Archbishop of Toledo, Fonseca, and the Grand Inquisitor, Manrique, were keen readers and admirers of Erasmus to whom Fonseca paid a pension of 200 ducats a year.

When Cervantes was born, the reaction caused in Spain by Luther's attack on the unity of the Church had set in; but if the brakes of orthodoxy had been pulled hard, the University was still a brilliant centre of learning and the city swarmed with boisterous and noisy students. Cervantes was not one of them, for he was born in a family both poor and numerous; but he did manage to acquire enough Latin to read the classics. That he was a voracious reader we know because he says so himself in his *Don Quixote* (1. ix.); 'I who am fond of reading even the scraps of paper lying about in the streets . . .'

This detail which he gives about himself throws much light on his character: we can see the bookish, reflective figure walking along with his dreamy eyes on the ground—for it is strange how dreamers look downwards and not upwards as it seems they should. The fact marks him at once as a man destined to blossom out at the end of the century, when the wave of the mind of Spain was to surge and rise as the wave of the will of Spain was breaking and sinking.

Yet there he was, a young, healthy man, and no

fortune; fond of poetry and a wistful admirer of Lope de Rueda, the actor-author who travelled from city to city setting his plays on a few planks supported by four barrels. From his youngest days, he felt in him that urge to imitate life which is the mark of the artist; but life had first to be lived; and what better theatre than that of Spain's many-sided historical adventures? Cervantes went to Italy.

The *Deus ex machina* in this case was a young Papal Legate in his early twenties, Cardinal Aquaviva, whom Philip II (displeased with Pope Pius V) had requested to leave Spain within sixty days. Aquaviva complied and Cervantes entered his household as steward. So it was that the youthful poet, at twenty-two, discovered that Italian world in which the Spaniards ruled the Italians and the Italians taught their masters to worship the Graces and the Muses. Cervantes' heart certainly was with the ruled, for he was a poet; and for him Italy was the Mecca of such prophets as Tasso and Ariosto, Boccaccio, Petrarch, and Dante; but he was in his twenties, and the call for a young Spaniard was still to action. In 1571 he had already enlisted in the famous Spanish troops known as the *Tercios*; and on October 7th (which might well be his birthday) in his 24th year, he fought in the naval battle of Lepanto, when the Grand Turk was defeated by Philip's half brother Don Juan of Austria.

He was ill with fever, but he could not remain in his dark bunk when the Sun of Victory was shining on the Christian Fleet; and so he fought and was wounded; and for the rest of his life, he was able to show his maimed left hand as a remembrance of what for him was 'the most glorious occasion the centuries ever saw'; for, as he was later to write in his *Voyage to Parnassus,*

> I had a share, though humble, in that victory.

After a number of other military adventures, in which he won more distinction than recognition, Cervantes left Italy for Spain in September 1575, well provided with letters from illustrious persons in Italy to illustrious persons in Madrid with a view to obtaining command of a company. These letters proved his undoing; for his ship was caught by pirates whose hopes of a fat ransom rose accordingly. He spent five years as a slave in Algiers.

This misfortune turned out to be the most fertile experience of his life. The circumstances were terrible, his masters, cruel. Two thousand lashes or death by barbarous means were daily occurrences. Hundreds, when not thousands of Christians, were kept in the notorious 'Baños', as raw material for ransom. Cervantes, still a young man of 28, took up at once the leadership of his brothers in exile. Several adventures in escape, conceived and led by him, ended in disaster through betrayal; but in every case, he, the leader came forward, and took upon himself all the responsibility and all the blame. In one case he refused to be ransomed alone; in another, with the fatal rope round his neck, he refused to add a single name or detail to his spontaneous self-accusation. His cool courage seems to have saved him from punishment. Greed for his ransom, or respect for his character, or a mixture of both, withheld the hand of the Venetian renegade from whose pleasure hung for five years the life of Cervantes and therefore the life of Don Quixote.

3

And who can doubt but that the seed of *Don Quixote* was planted in the spirit of Cervantes while he was a captive in Algiers? Of all the aspects of the situation, of all the flavours of that experience, one is bound to have sunk deeper than the others in his keen and sensitive soul: *he was a slave but he was a king*. There, in chains, by standing up to his executioners, he could command respect; by expecting nothing, begging nothing, he could rise to a position of moral independence and freedom such as few men can enjoy. In the Prisons of Algiers, Cervantes tasted that feeling of plenitude seldom granted: *complete moral sovereignty*.

Now, the key to his inner biography surely is that from the day he was ransomed he recovered his liberty and lost his sovereignty. In Algiers he had experienced five years of physical slavery and moral freedom; back in Spain, he had still to live thirty-six years of physical freedom and moral slavery.

For the rest of his life he had to live in the presence and company of this contrast: his inner worth, as a soldier and a Spaniard; his utter failure to get recognition for it. He might have incarnated examples of manliness and leadership in slavery; in liberty, he lived a life of helplessness and poverty; a king of infinite space in his Algerian cell, he was on the roads and in the inns and boarding houses of Spain but a scribbler of petitions to the King's ministers and of dedications and laudatory epistles to the King's grandees.

He lived still a few years of soldiering, part of them perhaps in Portugal; and had an amorous intrigue, possibly with a Portuguese woman, which loaded him with the care of a daughter without the advantages of a home; and in 1584 he married a Castillian woman, with a small property in Esquivias. There is a tradition that his wife is impersonated in Galatea, the heroine of the pastoral novel he published in the year of the marriage.

Why a pastoral novel? Because Cervantes was above all so rich in invention that he accepted without demur the forms he found in his time. Two other Europeans come to mind in this connection: Shakespeare and Mozart, both of whom take forms as they find them (Shakespeare even the plots) and are content to pour their rich wine into the old bottles. In this his first literary adventure, however, Cervantes was too trustful; the pastoral novel was dead or dying. His *Galatea* was not a success and he had to struggle on. He wrote for the theatre, in Spain a voracious monster in his time, for the public wanted new comedies every day; but in the end he had to seek sustenance in other than literary pursuits, and became a purveyor for the Armada, and later a tax collector. He managed to earn an excommunication in his first capacity, for having dared to commandeer wheat belonging to the Church; and to go to jail in his second, for his unorthodox accountancy. In between, he had petitioned the King for a post in the Indies, then in his own words 'the refuge and shelter of all the Spaniards who have lost hope'. 'Let him find something here'—was the royal answer. He did find something. *Don Quixote*.

4

As a personal creation, as a flower of experience, *Don Quixote* is the outcome of that contrast between the majesty of Cervantes as a slave in Algiers and his misery as a free man in Spain. That fall of his from the castle of dignified slavery to the dirt-track of wandering freedom is the origin of all the falls of the Knight of the Doleful Countenance.

But by then the individual experience of Algiers had widened and deepened into an experience that was national in its scope. Born under Charles V, a Knight Errant whose Dulcinea had been the unity of Europe under the unity of the Faith, Cervantes had lived under Philip II, a Sancho Panza ever scribbling the niggardly accounts of his short-sighted policies. Cervantes, who had lost the use of his left hand in the battle of Lepanto, lived to see Lope de Vega return from the defeat of the Armada; and he, who knew the Spanish roads as no one has known them before or since, must have observed the state of things which, at the time, the Spanish Ambassador in London, Gondomar, described to the King in these words: 'There are neither beds nor inns nor meals, owing to the many taxes and vexations that weigh on your subjects'. Here again, the Knight had fallen into the dust; and the experience must have been deep and grave.

But the greatness of the book does not come merely from this twofold experience: it comes from the spirit of the man who transmuted it. Had Cervantes been less great, the theme would have been marred by bitterness. Now, that which makes this story—fantastic though it is—so much like a piece of reality is the serene impartiality of its mood; the universal love of human beings, sympathy with their foibles, understanding of their lives, which animates the whole picture and allows every man and woman in it to be himself or herself on his or her own merits and stand on his own feet in his own way.

5

Rich as his invention was, a prodigious capacity for creating types and situations was not the greatest gift of Cervantes. Though lacking the graces and the lyrical warmth of Lope de Vega, the verbal alchemy of Góngora, the metaphysical flights of Calderón, Cervantes is the greatest poet of Spain, for he is the roomiest, largest, and richest soul Spain has given forth. Consciously, he was perhaps (I am not sure) a faithful child of the Church. But all his magnanimous tendencies make of him as free a thinker as Shakespeare, and more generous and sensitive to human suffering than that distant English aristocrat. We know he was sly and ironical, for he told us so himself:

I, a sly man, old poet cured by age,

he says in his *Voyage to Parnassus*; and so we have a right to read him between the lines. Read then this: Sancho and Don Quixote meet the peasants who are conveying the images of St. George, St. Martin, St. James, and St. Paul; whereupon, Don Quixote explains to Sancho the deeds of the four Holy Knights, and of St. Martin, he says: 'I believe he was even more liberal than brave, as you may gather, Sancho, from this sight, since he is sharing his cloak with the poor man, giving him half of it.' Things might have ended there, had the pen been wielded by any other Spaniard of his century; but the writer is Cervantes, and so he lends to Don Quixote a sly, ironical comment: 'and, no doubt, this must have happened in winter, for otherwise,

he would have given away the whole cloak, he was so
charitable'.

To smile and read on will not do. We must take in
the human, liberal intention behind those words, not
perhaps hostile but certainly foreign to the rigid orthodoxy of the century. One does not imagine Lope or
Calderón or even Quevedo writing in such a vein. Nor
is the story at an end. What has Sancho to say on hearing his master's explanation? 'Perhaps it was not what
you say, Sir; but rather that he (St. Martin) stuck to our
proverb that to *give away and yet hold on requires a
head that's well screwed on.*'

This quiet, almost invisible smile, holds the reader
time and again. The humour of Cervantes is ever
aroused whenever he has to deal with clerics; usually,
though, in a quiet, almost silent way. When Sancho
swaps his donkey's packsaddle for the more luxurious
one of the Barber's (he who had lost Mambrino's helmet in battle with Don Quixote) how does Cervantes
himself, for it is he who is speaking, describe the opera-
tion? 'Sancho'—he writes—'performed *mutatio cap-
parum*', and not a word more about it. But the Latin
words refer to the change over of the capes worn by
cardinals which usually takes place in Rome on Resur-
rection Day; and before the reader has caught his meaning, Cervantes is talking about something else. For
those in whose minds a doubt might linger as to the
deliberate character of this parallel between donkeys
and cardinals, here is another scene. It belongs to that
marvellous story of the braying aldermen who went
each his way around the hill braying now and then in
the hope of finding an ass one of them had lost; and they
brayed so perfectly that they mutually deceived each

other into thinking that the other one was the actual ass until in the end they met face to face full of admiration for each other's powers; and they vied in mutual praises until one of them closed the tournament with a most tendentious proverb: 'If the abbot sings well, the choir boy need not feel envious.'

Is the intention clear? And must it not have been fairly strong to come out so forcibly in that era of strict orthodoxy? To be sure, a fiercer form of attack against priests, nuns, and friars can be found in Quevedo; but in this outspoken satirist, the force of the onslaught is aimed at the sins of the clergy, as a moral weapon; not as in Cervantes played on the clergy as an intellectual game.

The smile of Cervantes is not, however, always merely mischievous and good humoured. At times it turns grave and sad. How bitter in its sobriety is that sentence in which Don Quixote presents to Sancho the image of St. James 'the Moor-killer'. 'Don Quixote . . . asked for another of the sheets to be removed, under which was seen the image of the Patron Saint of the Spains, on horseback, his sword red with blood, riding over Moors and treading over human heads. "This is the Knight of Knights, and the squadrons of Christ; his name is Don Saint James the Moor-killer, one of the most valiant saints and knights the world ever owned and now Heaven owns".' Let those who will still hold that the words 'treading over human heads', followed by that 'this is the Knight of Knights and of the squadrons of Christ' were written with no particular intention bear in mind the contrast between Cervantes' presentation of St. James and that of St. Paul: 'This was the greatest enemy the Church of God our Lord had in his time, and her greatest defender she will ever have; a Knight Errant in life and a Saint on foot in his death; an untirable worker in the Lord's vineyard, doctor of men, who had Heavens for his schools and Jesus Christ himself as a professor and teacher.' The opposition between St. James—cruelty, arms—and St. Paul—charity, letters—could not be more striking.

And what can we say about his sad and grave smile when relating Sancho's meeting with the Morisco? Just after he had left the government of his Island, Sancho met Ricote, a Spanish Morisco expelled like his brethren by Philip III's Decree, and like his brethren returned to Spain illegally, for, as Cervantes makes him say, 'sweet is the love of one's mother country'. The whole page is a hardly concealed protest against the cruelty of the expulsion; in the course of which Ricote, the Morisco, lets fall this: 'I arrived in Germany, and there it seemed to me one could live with more freedom; for the inhabitants do not look into many fine points; everyone lives as he wishes, for in the largest part of it one lives in full freedom of conscience.'

Despite a few shielding sentences or words here and there, this episode must be read as a protest against the cruelty and inhumanity of the expulsion. But of whose expulsion? No doubt that of the Moriscoes, which was more recent; but does he not mean also, mainly perhaps, that of the Jews? No little caution is required in forming an opinion on what Cervantes says, silences, or suggests; but his words should be weighed and carefully scrutinized. How could we pass in unobservant indifference over his curious attitude towards the old Christian, the status in which those with no Jewish or Moorish blood took so much (un-Christian) pride?

Cervantes hardly ever mentions it without a slightly mocking, ironic, or sarcastic intention; and he is wont to bring it in as a boastful utterance on the part of coarse, mean, and uneducated persons. 'From such tears and such an honest determination on the part of Sancho Panza, the author of this history gathers that he must have been well born and at least an old Christian.' The irony is obvious, and twice ironical if it be remembered that the author of the story was supposed to be a Moor. But is this the tone of the Spaniards of those days?

In his sketch *The Election of the Mayors of Daganzo*, one of the candidates, Humillos, asked whether he can read, gives this somewhat terrific answer:

> Certainly not. Nor will't ever be proved
> that in my lineage there was a single person
> senseless enough to learn such a chimaera
> as reading, good for nothing but to drive
> men to the stake and women to the brothel.

And this Humillos, who boasts in such forthright terms of being unable to read, adds the following lines:

> With this, and being as I am an old Christian
> I make bold to be as good as a Roman senator.

His rival Jarrete is not to be outdone; and after describing his activities, such as ploughing and shoeing young bulls, he adds:

> I am healthy in my limbs, I do not ail
> with deafness or cataract, or rheumatism or
> cough,
> and I am an old Christian like everybody
> and can shoot with a ball as well as Tullius.

Here is another case: 'In one word, they are farmers, plain people with no mixture whatsoever of any ill-sounding race, and, as the saying goes, rancid old Christians; but so rich that their wealth and magnificent style of living is gradually winning for them the name of *hidalgos* and even of knights.' Curious, isn't it? Why that *but?* And why so much discretion about that 'ill-sounding race'? Or again, these words of Sancho: '. . . and when I had nothing else (in my favour) but to believe, as I firmly and truly do, in God and in everything the Holy Roman Catholic Church holds and believes in, and to be a deadly enemy of the Jews . . .' Is it possible to read such passages without gathering to which side Cervantes leant? And his jokes? Are they in tune with his epoch and country? Do they not delve deeper than those of the sarcastic, satirical, biting but orthodox Quevedo? Would an old Christian in seventeenth-century Spain exclaim, as Sancho does, in praise of the wine he has just swallowed with delight: 'Oh the whoreson, and how Catholic he is, the scoundrel!' Would an old Christian author lend to one of his characters that even bolder exclamation which Cervantes makes Sansón Carrasco utter: 'Pray Almighty God where He is at his longest . . .' Such passages abound in which this universal spirit, free from the fetters of space and time, smiles, laughs, and guffaws under his cloak.

No suspicion of oversubtlety need therefore attach to an interpretation that would see a deliberate allusion to the Inquisition in the following scene: the Duke and Duchess have staged an open-air entertainment to last through the night, with much noise, artillery, bonfires burning everywhere. Sancho, deeply disturbed through it all, is at last happy to hear some music in the distance, and he says to the Duchess: 'My lady, where there is music there can be no bad thing.' 'Nor where there are lights and clarity,' the Duchess answers. Whereupon, Sancho replies: 'There is light in a fire, and clarity in blazes, as we see in those that surround us and might very well burn us to ashes.'

'Surround *us*.' Might very well burn *us*. Whom does this 'us' stand for? On the surface, it refers to Sancho, to the Duchess, and to those who happen to be about in the wood at the time; but in the cellar of the hidden sense, is it not possible to suspect that Cervantes meant to refer to a concrete, unmentioned 'us'? Let these and many other pages of Cervantes in the same vein be read bearing in mind that he himself lends to one of his characters (Mauricio in *Persiles and Sigismunda*) these significant words: 'I followed the ways of my country, at any rate those which seemed to be level with reason; and as for those that were not, I made a show to follow them with feigned appearances, for dissimulation may at times be profitable.'

Could he have said it more clearly. Yes. He could and did: 'The hypocrite who feigns to be good does less harm than the public sinner'; so he declares in *Don Quixote*. Or again: 'Simulated holiness does harm to no third person; only to the person who uses it.' And let no one forget that this Cervantes who sets down such abstract and general pleadings in favour of hypocrisy is the same who managed so neatly to make Sancho confess in a general and abstract way the concrete and particular sin against his master which he had committed by forging an imaginary incantation of Dulcinea.

Whither all this? Is it possible to consider Cervantes as a representative Spaniard of his epoch? Are his ideas

similar to those then current in Spain? Listen to the cry
of Marcela, the young rich shepherdess, before the dead
body of her stubborn though rejected lover: 'I was
born free, and in order to be able to be free, I chose the
solitude of the fields.' Is this not already the voice of
the eighteenth century and of Rousseau? The arguments Don Quixote brandishes to induce the Knight of
the Green Coat to let his son study whatever the young
man wishes, are they not already our modern ideas
on education, founded on a more respectful attitude
towards human nature than Cervantes' epoch ever
knew? In Marcela's speech, so full of substance, this
sentence will be found, a philosophy in itself: '. . . and
just as the viper does not deserve to be accused for its
poison, though it kills with it, since that poison was
given it by nature, so I should not be censured for being
beautiful.' Is there anything in this attitude that
recalls Calderón, Lope, or Quevedo?

What are we then to make of this spirit of freedom
in the thought of Cervantes? (I am not speaking of free
thought in Cervantes, which would be an anachron-
ism.) What of his mocking attitude towards the clergy,
his hardly veiled hints about the Inquisition, his protest
against the expulsion of the Moriscoes, and, at least by
implication, of the Jews; his ironical attitude towards
the pride of the old Christians? Let the specialized
scholars answer. Perhaps the time may have come to
direct research towards a possible Sephardi origin of
Cervantes. Among many pointers, none fully convincing, yet impressive in the aggregate, here is one: He is
relating how he found in Toledo the story of *Don
Quixote* written in Arabic; and goes on to say: 'And
it was not difficult to find a translator, for even if I had

B

looked for one from a better and older language, I should have found him.' It is fairly obvious that he is thinking of Hebrew; but why so discreet? Does it not recall that other discretion: 'Without any mixture whatsoever of an ill-sounding race'? And why a *better* language? Let the profession and the wandering life of Cervantes' father be borne in mind. Read again that moving Preface to *Persiles* and the dedication written as he himself says 'with a foot in the stirrup' for he is on his death-bed, and carefully weigh the words in it and those that are not there, such as *sin, salvation, God . . .*; consider the state of mind of this dying man who knows he is dying, and ask yourself if an old Christian Spaniard dying in 1616 could have said farewell to the world with such a supreme but pagan serenity.

6

This serenity in the face of death was ever Cervantes' attitude towards life. As he says himself in his *Voyage to Parnassus*, 'for disparity, the gates of my mind are never opened; for consonance, always'. He was, therefore, a liberal in our own modern sense of the word, a man who seeks harmony and concordance in all things. He was one of the minds of his time—Francis Bacon was another—who guessed in Nature some immanent wisdom from which man could only stray at his risk. He was the herald of the era of reason.

The three great books, *Gargantua*, *The Essays*, and *Don Quixote* are as three milestones on the road the European spirit covered from the knightly epoch illustrated by the two great European monarchs towards our modern days. But how rich their differences and shades! Rabelais, still medieval, ends and liquidates the Middle Ages. Montaigne, a critical rather than a creative mind, draws the chief lines of the human spirit with an objectivity free from the fetters of time. Of the three, Cervantes is the most genuine herald of our time, the true forerunner of modern man.

Freed from their respective roots and skies, considered only in that intellectual space in which their outlines stand out in all their purity, Rabelais, Montaigne, and Cervantes rise in Europe like the three caryatides which support our epoch. In this intellectual space, it is possible to envisage Cervantes as a Rabelais purified by Montaigne, a Montaignized Rabelais. No direct historical connection is suggested, since Cervantes knew neither Rabelais nor Montaigne; but only absolute and positional relations, one might almost say geometrical relations between three forms of the human spirit.

In its creative impulse, *Don Quixote* springs up with a vertical vigour similar to that which animates the immense work of Rabelais. In both cases we are struck by a similar volcanic independence from the social and moral layers deposited by the past; a similar primitive force of a creation flowing from deeper levels and rising to higher levels than those of ordinary, everyday life. In this sense, considered as explosive (or as a geologist would say) crystalline artists, Cervantes and Rabelais go hand in hand. There is an exorbitant quality in Don Quixote's gestures and words which brings him close to Gargantua and Pantagruel. Just like Rabelais' heroes, the hero of Cervantes breaks all frameworks and bursts all forms.

But here ends the likeness between them. From

Rabelais to Cervantes, a whole generation has elapsed; and in those days evolution was almost as rapid as in ours. When Cervantes comes of age, the Middle Ages are dead. The picturesque chivalries of Charles V and Francis I were no more than stage refinements, idealized memories of a bygone reality which in itself had lacked neither brutality nor roughness. This roughness and this brutality still overshadow and load with sombre heaviness the pages full of kitchen salt and shameless laughter poured from his fertile brain by the priest-doctor of Chinon.

All this cramming with food, swilling with drink, piling of refuse, flooding of words, the very enormity of the characters, all this bursts with a lack of measure at first sight unexpected from a French genius. A fascinating paradox: Don Quixote stands as far out beyond measure as Gargantua and Pantagruel; but Cervantes succeeds where Rabelais fails or does not try to succeed: in keeping a sense of proportion even beyond the bounds of measure.

Cervantes also deals in giants. But with how delightful a smile. ' "How big does Your Mercy think, my Sir Don Quixote," the Barber asked, "the Giant Morgante might be?" ' A question, be it noted, which is in itself a bridge between the Middle Ages (giants) and our own times (how big?). And our Knight answers with such a treasure of shadings, and so mischievously dosified, that in his answer can already be perceived glimmers of the smiles of Voltaire and guesses of the discoveries of Cuvier. 'In this business of giants, there are different opinions as to whether giants existed at all in the world or not; but Holy Writ, which cannot stray one atom from truth, shows us that they existed, when it tells us the history of that huge Philistine Goliath who was seven and a half cubits tall, which is a disproportionate height. In the Island of Sicily, shin-bones and spines have been found, so big that their very size proves their owners to have been giants as big as towers, for geometry puts this truth beyond doubt. Withal, I should not be able to say for certain how big Morgante was, although I imagine that he cannot have been very tall; and I am drawn to this view by reading in the history in which a special mention is made of his deeds that he slept many times under a roof; so that, since he found houses big enough to hold him, his bigness cannot have been out of the common.'

How masterly the handling of light and shade, of smile and earnestness and slyness! We have wandered far from that cavern in Chinon, that cyclopean forge in whose dark recesses the physician-friar, a monastic Jupiter, a Faculty-Vulcan, forged his cardboard-and-glue giants under the noise of cataracts of laughter and the thunder of oaths. From the one to the other, Montaigne has passed over the world. The kitchen salt has been dissolved in the pure water of thought, decanted in solitude, become subtler. Movements are still powerful and exorbitant; but the violence which threatened every instant to upset the balance of the whole has vanished; and in its place an intellectual order reigns quietly and unobtrusively, keeping every part linked and disciplined to the whole. Even giants must be inserted into this order, and, instead of incarnating the anarchy of a medieval era in a state of disintegration, they take their appointed place in the new order as objects for study, doubtful beings for free opinion, articles of faith for the believer, natural entities subject to the laws of geometry for the man of science, data offered for observation to the honest and curious man. So that, while Rabelais attacks the Middle Ages staging it as an outsize caricature of itself, Cervantes turns away from it casting on life a clear and serene glance.

What a singular achievement it was making wisdom glow out of the deeds of a lunatic, opening the modern age with the exploits of a knight-errant who spurns fire-arms, and attaining universal fame under the guise of killing a literary form already dying! For what makes of *Don Quixote* a living and enduring book, a kind of Bible of the western spirit, is that the core of the work, the heart in it which beats steadily under the in-coherent emotion of the sublime and absurd hero, is no other than the problem of all men and of all centuries, yet more particularly, our own problem, that of the westerners, namely: what is truth?

Truth, Don Quixote affirms, is a revealed or dreamt thing: everything the soul wishes, if it really does wish it. Truth is the creative principle of reality; but, once created, reality withstands new truths. Therefore, noble truths must be protected from debased reality; or, in other words, the reality of tomorrow must be protected from that of today. And Sancho replies: Truth is a sum of things and happenings which one causes or experiences, and which leave as their dregs a lot of proverbs. Man hardly ever sees anything beyond his nose, but that is better than nothing; and with the help of memory he may add inch by inch to the dregs of things and happenings left by the men of yesterday, so as to make up a fund of proverbs or common sense.

7

If then Cervantes occupies in the History of Europe and perhaps of mankind the eminent place which the whole world grants to him, it is because, under the poet who gave to the world Don Quixote, Sancho, and the rest, lives a philosopher open to all the mysteries of the human spirit. By no means, however, a mere rationalist; witness his remark on nonsense:

Can nonsense please unless it comes deliberately
Led in by wit?

No one ever ran Irish bulls more felicitously. Here is an example from *Don Quixote*: 'Those maidens who, with whip and palfrey, and with all their maidenhood about them wandered from hill to hill, from dale to dale, so that unless a rogue or a villain in axe and helmet, or a boisterous giant ravished them, maidens there were in past ages who, after eighty years during which they never slept under a roof, went to their grave as pure virgins as the mothers who bore them.'

This pleasure he found in nonsense deliberately brought in by wit is both a proof and a guarantee of a freedom beyond and above mere rationalism. Here the roots are hidden of his inimitable humour, a humour that blossoms only in the heights open to all the winds of the spirit, equally capable of laughter and of gravity, and of that grave serenity which outlives and conquers the worst and most tenacious adversity. The master-piece of this lofty yet simple and even modest mood is the Preface he wrote a few days before his death for his last book, *Persiles*. But there is one other page, less quoted and equally wise in his *Voyage to Parnassus*. He has described all the poets he cared to remember seated around Apollo, points out that he is left standing and complains to the god. He enumerates his merits and his works, then goes on :

> Against my dreary lot, I do not rave;
> Though, seeing myself unseated, as I do,
> And in this place, I do my grievance rue.
> With little I can do, though much I crave.

And he makes the god answer him :

> You have yourself contrived your own hard lot;
> And I betimes have seen you fortunate;
> But fortune, with the foolish, tarries not.
> Yet if you would your life and grievance fit
> Not abashed, but well comforted and gay,
> Fold your own cape and on your cape do sit.

The poet's humour, however, claims the last word :

> 'Tis plain, my lord, that no one has yet hit
> On this : I have no cape on which to sit.

And so he stands for ever in Parnassus, unruffled, capeless, and free.

Cervantes and Chivalry Books

IT is a commonplace that *Don Quixote* was written in order to oust from the world of books the Romances of Chivalry. We have Cervantes' own word for it: first and last. First, in the Prologue itself:

> And since this your work aims at nothing but at undoing the authority and welcome which Chivalry Books enjoy with the world and the vulgar . . .

Last, in the very closing sentence of the story:

> For my object has been no other than to make men abhor the made-up and extravagant stories of Chivalry Books, which, through those of my true *Don Quixote*, are beginning to totter and without doubt will ultimately fall.

Yet it would take more than one quotation to give a complete impression of Cervantes' real attitude towards Books of Chivalry—certainly more complex and probably less unfavourable than his professed intention in writing *Don Quixote* would lead us to believe.

Comic writers were ever shamefaced and apologetic, and Rabelais himself advises the reader to look between the lines for the *substantifique moêlle* of his teachings. Mankind is so overburdened with cares that it feels it almost sinful to laugh and must seek for moral and even physical pretexts to excuse a hearty enjoyment of the light side of life. Hence the dictum *Castigat ridendo mores*, in which *ridendo*, being a somewhat disreputable word, is smuggled in between two perfectly respectable worthies—*castigat* and *mores*. This was ever true, but it was never truer than during the period which stretches between the crumbling down of the classical and the completion of modern civilization.

The Middle Ages knew no clear distinction between the aesthetic, the scientific, and the moral. For them learning is one and indivisible. Moreover, it usually comes from the clerics, guardians of the moral law. For at first all learning was religious, and even when lay intellectual interests began to flourish learned men had to support themselves by church appointments, just as nowadays most learned men support themselves by journalism. Hence, just as nowadays all writing seeks to justify itself by a political *raison d'être*, so in the Middle Ages all writing had to justify itself from a moral, or didactic point of view. Though the spirit was already abroad which was to replace it, this tradition still lived at the time of Cervantes—especially in Spain, owing to the austere tendencies which had grown in serious minds at the inspiration of the Counter-Reformation. Cervantes therefore feels bound to prove to his readers that he is not wasting time in endowing the world with one of its most precious treasures. Yet it is difficult to believe that the first impulse to which we owe such a splendid creation was merely critical, and of no great importance at that. On the face of it, *Don Quixote* was born in the exhilarating mood of inspiration, the only force capable of raising Cervantes' spirit above the miserable conditions to which he had then sunk. In the opening words of the Prologue, he says that *Don Quixote* 'was conceived in a prison, where all discomforts keep their residence and all dismal noises their habitation'. These words have given rise to many a learned discussion as to where, when, and in which prison *Don Quixote* was conceived. For our present purpose, it is enough to take the sentence in its symbolical sense, for while writing his masterpiece

Cervantes was imprisoned in the most dismal prison of all—that of dire poverty. Now it is hardly conceivable that from such a wretched cell of destitution Cervantes should have been lifted to the free spheres from which he writes by a mere desire to do away with the vogue for Books of Chivalry.

The matter may be further illustrated by a close examination of Cervantes' real opinions on Chivalry Books. It is well to remember that in Cervantes, as in almost every other Spanish genius, there is a pronounced lack of harmony between the critical and the creative faculties. As a creator, Cervantes is one of the freest men of genius in the world of art. As a critic, his mind is both guided and fettered by classical and academic ideas which merge into hard literary dogmas, as it were, without warning. The two tendencies appear almost inextricably mixed in his attitude towards Books of Chivalry.

AS A CRITIC

We observe from the very outset that Cervantes objects to Chivalry Books on the ground of their style. He quotes the extravagant arabesques of Feliciano de Silva : 'The reason of the unreason which to my reason is meted out in such wise my reason doth enfeeble that it is with good reason that I complain of your beauty,' or 'the high heavens that of your divinity divinely fortify you with the stars, make you meritorious of the merit which your greatness has merited'.

Having thus laid down the theme, he will often embroider on it and make this extravagant complication the butt of his satire—direct, as in this page, or indirect, as in the numerous passages where he makes

Don Quixote imitate the elaborate style of *Amadís*. His objection to this style is twofold; Cervantes stands as the champion of simplicity against both affectation and complication.

As with style, so with substance. Cervantes dislikes Books of Chivalry because they lack truth. His constant reproach is that they are 'lying' and 'false' ('mentirosos', 'falsos'). But he seems to take these words in more than one sense. Let us hear him through the mouth of the Canon of Toledo:

'Truly, Master Curate, in my opinion, these they call Books of Chivalry are very harmful to the community; and though, led by an idle and false taste, I have read the beginning of almost all of them that have appeared in print, I never was able to read any one through to the end; for to me they all seem to be the same, little more, little less, and this one has in it nothing more than that one, and your one than the rest. It appears to me that this kind of writing and composition must be classed along with that of the fables which are called Milesian, which are extravagant stories aiming purely at pleasure and not at instruction, contrary to what is the case with the fables called apologies, which seek both to instruct and to please. And though the main purpose of such books is to please, I fail to see how they can attain it, being filled with so many extravagancies, and so outrageous; for the pleasure which our soul conceives must rise from the beauty and harmony which it sees or beholds in the things which the sight or the imagination lay before it; and things which in themselves bear uglyness and disproportion cannot produce in us any pleasure whatever. For what beauty can there be, or what proportion of the parts to the whole and of the whole to the parts in a book or tale wherein a boy of sixteen years of age at one cut of his sword cleaves a giant as tall as a steeple through the middle as easily as if he were made of sugar paste? Or when they want to relate a battle to us, and after having stated that the enemy is one million strong, if only the hero of the book is against them, we are forced to understand that the said knight attained victory by the mere virtue of his mighty arm? And what are we to say of the ease with which a queen or an heir-empress delivers herself into the hands of a knight errant and unknown? What mind, unless altogether barbarous and uncultivated can find any pleasure in reading that a great tower, full of knights, cuts through the sea like a ship with favourable wind, and to-night sees the sunset in Lombardy and to-morrow the dawn in the land of Prester John or in some other land never described by Ptolemy nor seen by Marco Polo? And if to this it were answered that the authors of such books compose them as men who avowedly write lies, and therefore are not bound to a nice respect for truth, I would retort that lies are the better as they more closely resemble truth, and the more pleasing as they contain more of the dubious and the possible. Lying fables should match the understanding of their readers, being so contrived that reconciling impossibilities, removing obstacles, keeping all minds in suspense, they may surprise, astonish, rejoyce and entertain in such wise that pleasure and wonder may proceed apace; and all these things are impossible to him who strays from the verisimilitude of imitation—wherein lies the perfection of what is written. I have never seen a Book of Chivalry the fable of which may be said to be an entire body, with all its members, and so that the middle corresponds to the beginning, and the end to the beginning and the middle; but rather are they composed with so many members that their authors seem to aim at forming a chimera or a monster, and not a well-proportioned figure. Moreover, they are harsh in their style, incredible in their exploits, licentious in their love-affairs, inconsiderate in their courtesies, prolix in their battles, silly in their arguments, nonsensical in their travels, and finally altogether wanting in skill, and therefore worthy of being banished from the Christian Commonwealth as a useless breed.' (Part I, Chapter xlvii.)

There are two or three layers of criticism here. There is first a criticism of Chivalry Books on the ground that they are not true in a literary sense, that is, that they lack verisimilitude. It is Cervantes' strongest ground. He objects to the extravagant imagination which pleased itself in fancying impossible situations. In this he is the representative of mere common sense. He banishes the miraculous out of fiction and would have 'lies' made as truthlike as possible. He notes that even Don Quixote had his doubts about 'the wounds which Don Belianis gave and received, for he imagined that, great as the masters might be who cured him, he must needs have his face and body covered with scars and traces'. He makes the Curate say of *Tirant the White*:

'In troth, my neighbour, this is the best book of its kind in the world; here, knights eat and sleep and die in their beds, and make their wills before dying, with other things which are lacking in other books of this type.' (Part I, Chapter vi.)

This is the reaction which Cervantes represents against the disregard for the material conditions in which men live in this world. And along with this claim, Cervantes puts forward the claims of human nature, often forgotten by the idealistic writer of Chivalry Romances. Thus, the passage in which he humorously extols Don Quixote in words which are an oblique satire on Chivalry Books:

. . . the first who in our age and in these calamitous times devoted himself to the labours and exertions of knight errantry, to righting wrongs, rescuing widows and protecting maidens—those maidens who, with whip and palfrey, and with all their maidenhood about them, wandered from hill to hill, from dale to dale, so that unless a rogue or a villain in axe and helmet, or a boisterous giant ravished them, maidens there were in past ages who, after eighty years during which they never had slept under a roof, went to their grave as pure virgins as the mothers who bore them. (Part I, Chapter ix.)

In the name of common sense, Cervantes here pulls down to earth the knight-errant who galloped in painted skies. He acts towards Books of Chivalry as Sancho does to Don Quixote; he is the advocate of the earth and the solid flesh, and the infinite shades of complexity of human nature. For idealists simplify, or rather, deal in 'simples', as do chemists, while we mortals have to live in a world of hopelessly entangled compounds. Thus, this first objection which Cervantes raises against Chivalry Books, being grounded in common sense, is at bottom an aesthetic objection, for there is no wider and more comprehensive view of nature and life than that of the artist, he who sees things as a whole.

This criticism, essentially of an instinctive and popular character, merges into one of a purely intellectual kind. Cervantes' second objection to Chivalry Books is that of a classic intellectual protesting against the wild and extravagant production of Romanticists. Let there be no mistake about it. The Canon of Toledo pours his Horatian scorn on those fables, not one of which 'may be said to be an entire body, with all its members, and so that the middle corresponds to the beginning and the end to the beginning and the middle, but rather are they composed with so many members that their authors seem to aim at forming a chimera or a monster, and not a well proportioned figure'. But while we willingly concur in this criticism, applied to

Chivalry Books, we may be led to forget that Cervantes would have passed exactly the same judgement on *Hamlet* and *King Lear*, had he known them. All readers of *Don Quixote* remember that the Canon and the Vicar naturally pass from the discussion of Books of Chivalry to that of the *Comedias* of the romantic type which the genius of Lope de Vega, helped and sustained by popular favour, had at last established on the Spanish Stage, against the classical preference of the 'selected few', *los escogidos*, as Cervantes says. The good Canon, who thought of writing a model Book of Chivalry, gave it up, discouraged by the success of such works 'without head or tail' as were the plays then held in esteem by the Spanish public and written because they paid. The Vicar fully agrees with the Canon in his condemnation of both *Comedias* and Chivalry Books:

'You have hit upon a subject, Sir, which has stirred up in me an old aversion I have for the plays now in use, which is not inferior to that I bear to books of knight errantry;'

an agreement which need cause no surprise, since these two chapters are mere exercises in ventriloquy on the part of Cervantes anxious to find an outlet for his feelings as an unhappy playwright eclipsed by Lope de Vega. There is much in this page to justify itself in our eyes; for, even if we judge the Spanish theatre of those days by the plays usually read today—those of the best authors—extravagance of an indefensible nature and of the wildest romantic character is not altogether lacking. Much of his criticism on this account is then a mere defence of simplicity and clearness. But the central idea of this passage is inspired by the pseudo-classical criterion which prevailed at that period among what Cervantes himself calls 'the selected few', *los escogidos*, in practically all the countries of western Europe. This passage is an episode in the long struggle between classics and 'independents' which ended in a classical victory in France and in an 'independent' victory in Spain and in England—that is, everywhere, in a victory for the innate genius of the people concerned. Cervantes shows himself in it a true disciple of Horace and Aristotle as seen by the learned academies of Italy and Spain, and reveals how artificial and academic is his conscious taste. His literary tenets are to true literature what the dry and bookish 'propositions' of medieval theologians are to true religion. He is in fact a rhetorician, and one can read between the lines that his ambition is to emulate the glories of learned Italy rather than to create for the world an eternal image of living Spain.

And then there is a third layer of criticism in Cervantes' attitude towards Chivalry Books. It is not clear, and it does not always appear on the surface, but seems always to qualify his pronouncements on the matter; I refer to his objection to Books of Chivalry on the ground of their lack of historical truth. Fiction and history were not in Cervantes' time so strictly separated as in ours. The Chronicles are a mixture of both, and the age read and wrote them with a blend of that instinctive and uncritical belief in tales traditionally told, and of that innocence, with which illiterate people listen to plays or to ballads, never doubting for one moment that events happened as represented or related. Poems of early civilizations are purely informative and people listened to them for the sake of the story, not for the sake of the poet's art in narrating it—a taste which develops later.

Traces of this utilitarian origin linger to this day among simple people. It still influenced even the learned in Cervantes' time, when the distinction was not yet clear between story and history. While historians like Mariana weave many a legendary tale into their narrative, poets and story-tellers seem to consider themselves as counterfeiters of reality. It is a perfectly irrational feeling, which lingers from the past and seldom manifests itself directly. But it comes out indirectly now and then, as when authors claim as a special merit that their story really did happen in actual fact. Wordsworth does not seem wholly free from this feeling. Thus, commenting on 'Goody Blake and Harry Gill', he says: 'I wished to draw attention to the truth, that the power of human imagination is sufficient to produce such changes even in our physical nature as might almost appear miraculous. The truth is an important one; the fact, for it is a *fact*, is a valuable illustration of it.' (Preface to *Lyrical Ballads*.) All authors of Romances of Chivalry take great care to explain to the reader the supposed origin of their narrative; how such an historian wrote the manuscript and how it was buried in a tomb or some equally awe-inspiring place, and found and rescued and interpreted by the painstaking 'editor'. Such a *mise en scène* became a tradition among writers of Chivalry Books. Cervantes imitated it in his *Don Quixote*—hence Cide Hamete Benengeli and the Arabic papers found in the Alcaná of Toledo. Now, this traditional feature of Chivalry Books was no mere bluff. It was—unconsciously, perhaps—inspired by the feeling under which the author of fiction worked, that his calling was less respectable than that of the chronicler of actual historic fact. The feeling is rampant all through *Don Quixote* and tends to obscure and confuse Cervantes' ideas towards Chivalry Books.

The attitude of the people in the matter, as shown by Cervantes in *Don Quixote*, is one of faith in the printed word—that most pathetic of modern faiths. It is admirably expressed by the Innkeeper :

'I tell thee, friend,' said the Curate, 'neither Felixmarte of Hircania nor Cirongilio of Thrace ever existed, nor any similar knights that books of chivalry mention; for those books are invented and composed by idle wits who wrote them so that as you say people might beguile the time, as your harvesters do while reading them; for I truly swear to you that there never were such knights in the world nor such exploits and absurd adventures ever happened.'

'That bone may do for another dog,' said the Innkeeper. 'As if I knew not how many ones there are in five and where my shoe pinches me! Pray Sir, do not try to feed me with child's pap, for I am no fool. Would you have me believe that the stories told in those good books are but lies and absurdities, when they are printed by permission of those Gentlemen of the Royal Council, as if they were people likely to allow the printing of so many lies and so many battles and enchantments that take one's sense away!' (Part I, Chapter xxxii.)

The same Innkeeper provides us with a sidelight on Cervantes' own attitude, when he declares that, of the four books found in his wallet, he prefers those which deal with the exploits of Don Felixmarte of Hircania and Don Cirongilio of Thrace to the History of the Great Captain Gonzalo de Córdoba and the Life of Diego Garcia de Paredes. The Curate expostulates—and we shall come back to this expostulation, for it is highly suggestive in itself—that the first two are 'lying books' while the last two relate the exploits of men who actually existed. Thus do we gather that Cervantes' case against Chivalry Books included the objection that they were not history. But it might be argued that he is not speaking directly in this passage. There is, however, a page in which Cervantes himself speaks, and in the same sense. Remember the beginning of Chapter v, Part i.

Seeing then that he [Don Quixote] could not move, he resolved to have recourse to his usual remedy, which was to bethink himself of some happening in his books; and his folly brought then to his memory that incident when Baldwin left wounded in the wood by Charles is found by the Marquis of Mantua—a story familiar to little children, not unknown to young men, enjoyed and even believed by old people and withal, not truer than the miracles of Mahomet.

Here, though applied to a Ballad and not to a Book of Chivalry, the criterion is clearly implied. But in point of fact, the historical prejudice against Chivalry Books, though unconsciously held, is so strong in Cervantes that it inspires even his vocabulary on the matter. In the critical pages scattered here and there in *Don Quixote* 'lies' mean 'works of imagination'. The same subconscious attitude lurks under the word *Fiction* applied to novels.

Thus, in conclusion, the critical attitude of Cervantes towards Chivalry Books seems to be inspired by an objection against their lack of truth, grounded on three more or less obscurely held ideas, feelings or prejudices: an aesthetic-empirical desire for common sense, clearness, and simplicity, both as to substance and style; a classical, or pseudo-classical, taste which shuns extravagance and exaggeration but hankers after academic rules and rhetorical finery; and an historical-didactical prejudice against made-up tales and inventions without foundations of actual fact.

AS A CREATIVE ARTIST

In his creative capacity, however, Cervantes was not so unfavourable towards Chivalry Books. His acuity of perception and his creative impartiality enabled him, despite his own critical bias, to note with admirable accuracy the strength and limits of their popularity. It will be remembered that there is not one person in the whole of *Don Quixote* who has not read them, or heard them read—save perhaps, curiously enough, Sancho, an exception which is not without significance. But he is careful to suggest a delicate gradation of attitudes among readers. The humble people stand uppermost in their free acceptance, open admiration, and unreserved enjoyment of Chivalry Books. Witness that exquisite scene which takes place at the Inn when the Curate happened to say that poor Don Quixote had lost his reason through reading Books of Chivalry: the Inn-keeper, though willing to laugh at Don Quixote and to toss Sancho on a blanket, was not ready to accept any slander, direct or indirect, on Chivalry Books; and so:

'I do not know how that could have been; for indeed, so far as I can see, there is no better reading in the world, and I have somewhere, among other papers, two or three of them, that really have kept me and many others alive; for in harvest-time many harvesters gather here in the heat of the day, and there is always one who can read among them who takes in his hands one of those books and more than thirty of us sit around him, and we listen to him with so much pleasure that he takes away all our cares. For my own part, when I hear the mighty and furious blows that Knight-Errants do strike, I feel like doing as much myself and I should like to go on listening for nights and days.'

'And I should like you did even as you say,' said the hostess, 'for I never have a peaceful moment in the house but when you are listening to a reader; for then you are so lost in the story that you do not think of quarrelling.'

'That is so,' said Maritornes, 'and by my troth I also am fond of hearing those things, for they are most pretty; and especially when they tell about the lady who is under the orange-trees, tenderly hugged by the Knight, and that a duenna is watching for them, meanwhile full of envy and in great anxiety—I say that all these tales are as sweet as honey.'

'And you, what think you of the matter, young Miss,' said the Priest, addressing the Innkeeper's daughter.

'I know not, sir, upon my soul,' she answered, 'I also listen, and truly, though I do not understand it, I find much pleasure thereat. But I do not enjoy the hard blows, which my father prefers, but rather the lamentations of the knights when absent from their love-ladies, for in truth they often make me cry, out of compassion for them.' (Part I, Chapter xxxii.)

The next stage is perhaps represented in the Barber, a type of the people, somewhat sophisticated by the exercise of a trade of almost professional dignity—is he not the village doctor?—as well as by his familiarity with the Curate. His taste for books seems rather acquired than inherent in his nature, for he informs the Curate that he owns a *Ludovico Ariosto* in Italian 'though he does not understand it'. His behaviour throughout the 'great and diverting scrutiny' of Don

Quixote's library is curious to watch. He follows, somewhat passively, and one would say, almost reluctantly, the inquisitorial directions for destruction which he receives from the Curate—yet, now and then, finds courage to protest. His first stroke is the rescuing of Amadís:

And the first which Master Nicholas put in his [the Curate's] hands was the *Amadís of Gaul*, in four volumes. And the Curate said : 'This seems rather mysterious, for as I have often heard, this book was the first Romance of Chivalry printed in Spain, and all others have taken their source and origin in it; and thus I am of opinion that, as the theologian of such a pernicious sect, it must without excuse be condemned to the fire.'
'Not at all,' cried the Barber, 'for I have also heard that it is the best of all the books of its kind, and therefore, being single in its art, it must be reprieved.' (Part I, Chapter vi.)

This time the Curate acquiesces, and so, though with more reserve, does he also when the Barber hesitatingly puts in a word for Don Belianis.

Curate: 'Therefore, save your better judgment, Master Nicholas, I suggest that this one [Palmerin of England] and Amadís be exempted from the fire; and all the rest, without any further inquiry, be destroyed.'
'No, my friend,' the Barber replied, 'for this one which I have found is the famous Don Belianis.'

The Barber will not try any more rescues. He is not confident enough. One feels, in the passive way with which he hands the book over to the Curate, that he would fain take up the defence if only he dared or knew how to present it, and so he merely passes the books with a bare mention of the title, and never a word of criticism. For, as Cervantes says, after making the Curate deliver a critical opinion on Chivalry Books:

The Barber approved every word of this, and held it to be true and shrewdly thought, for he was convinced that the Curate was so good a christian and so great a friend of truth, that he would be unable to speak aught else for all the world.

So with the Barber we observe how the free instinctive pleasure in Chivalry Books begins to be repressed under an intellectual authority from above. A step higher, and we find Cardenio and Dorothea murmuring contemptuous remarks on the Innkeeper for his simplicity in believing in the actual existence of Don Felixmarte de Hircania and Don Cirongilio de Tracia.

On hearing this, Dorothea says to Cardenio in a low voice:
'There is little that our host needs to play second part to Don Quixote.'
'So I see,' answered Cardenio, 'for it is plain he believes that everything these books tell happened exactly as it is related in them, and not all the barefooted friars in the world will persuade him otherwise.' (Part I, Chapter xxxii.)

Now, this very Cardenio read *Amadís de Gaul*, and lent his own copy to his fiancée, Luscinda, who 'was very fond of Chivalry Books' and had asked him to send her one. And it will be remarked that this circumstance was responsible for the abrupt end of the first meeting between Cardenio and Don Quixote in Sierra Morena. For as soon as Cardenio, who is telling Don Quixote the story of his misfortunes, comes to mention *Amadís de Gaul*, and how Luscinda enjoyed it, Don Quixote forgets his promise to keep silent until the end of the relation, in order to bestow glowing praise on Luscinda's taste. Now, this very Cardenio who, when sane, laughs in his sleeve at the Innkeeper's credulity, having sunk into himself at Don Quixote's interruption, suddenly emerges with this extraordinary and utterly unexpected infatuation:

'I cannot drive this thought from my mind, nor can any man alive drive it from my mind, nor can any man make me think otherwise, and he is a fool who thinks or believes the reverse, that the arrant knave Elisabad was intimate with Queen Madasima.' (Part I, Chapter xxiv.)

Cardenio here is mad. Yes. But madness does not create *ex-nihilo*, and in choosing this particular way of presenting the unfortunate lover in his fit of fury, Cervantes reveals an admirable insight—probably due to his own personal experience—into the complexity of the attitude of well-educated people towards Books of Chivalry, with its mixture of conscious contempt and unconscious interest. The Curate, the Curate himself who acted as Inquisitor in Don Quixote's library, is not wholly free from a certain ill-repressed interest in Chivalry Books. The very paragraph in which Cervantes introduces both him and the Barber is to let us know that:

[Don Quixote] 'used often to discuss with the priest of his parish (who was a learned man, and a graduate of Sigüenza) as to who was the better knight, Palmerin of England or Amadís de Gaul.' (Part I, Chapter i.)

Great as was his wrath against Chivalry Books on account of their effect on Don Quixote's health, the Curate delivers himself of some strange opinions on them during the great and pleasant scrutiny: thus his judgement on Tirant the White is, to say the least, confused and almost self-contradictory, as of a man who cannot make up his mind. The books falls at the feet of the Barber who, anxious to have done with the work, had gathered a good armful to hand them over to the Housekeeper :

'God help me,' cried the Priest, aloud. 'Tirant the White here! Let me have it, my friend, for in it I reckon I have found a treasure of delight and a mine of recreation. Here is Don Kirieleison de Montalban, a valiant knight, and his brother, Thomas de Montalban, and the knight Fonseca, and the battle which the brave Tirant fought with the mastiff, and the witty sayings of the damsel Placerdemi-vida, and the loves and wiles of the widow Reposada, and the Empress in love with Hipolito, the squire. In truth, my neighbour, this is the best book of its kind in the world; here, knights eat and sleep and die in their beds, and make their wills before dying, with other things which are lack-ing in other books of this type. And yet I assure you that he who contrived it, inasmuch as he did not mean all the nonsense he wrote, deserved to be sent to the galleys for life. Take it home and read it, and you will see that all I say is true.' (Part I, Chapter vi.)

The Curate's liking for chivalry tales, here concealed under jesting and criticism, bursts frankly forth when the Barber comes upon the two Palmerins—of Oliva and of England: though he condemns the first, he waxes lyrical in his praise of the second:

'Let that Olive be cut in slices and burnt, so that not even its ashes remain; and let that Palm of England be kept and preserved as a thing that stands alone, and a box be made for it such as that which Alexander found among the spoils of Darius, and which he thought worthy of holding Homer's works. This book, my good neighbour, derives its authority from two causes; the first because it is very good in itself; and the second, because tradition has it that it was written by a wise king of Portugal. All the adventures of the Castle of Miraguarda are excellent and of charitable contrivance, and the dialogue is polished and clear, and such that the station of the person who speaks is observed and respected with great propriety and judgment.' (Part I, Chapter vi.)

This is hardly the language of an Inquisitor on heretical books. But there is yet another passage in which the Curate reveals how much in tune he is with the world of Chivalry Books. It is one of those truly Cervantian passages where humour is so subtle and so deep that one is left wondering how much of it Cervantes meant to put there. It occurs in that same Chapter xxxii, so often quoted, in the course of the discussion between the Curate and the Innkeeper on the merits and trustworthiness of Chivalry Books.

'My friend,' said the Curate, 'these two books [*Don Felixmarte de Hircania* and *Don Cirongilio de Tracia*] are untrue and are full of vagaries and absurdities while that other book of the Great Captain is true history and tells the deeds of Gonzalo Hernandez de Cordoba, who on account of his great and numerous exploits deserved to be called by the whole world the Great Captain, famous and honourable surname which he was alone to deserve : and this Diego García de Paredes was a notable knight, born in the city of Trujillo, in Estremadura, a soldier of extraordinary courage and of such mighty strength that he could stop a mill-wheel in all its fury with one finger; and, once, standing at the entrance of a bridge with just his broadsword, he withstood the onslaught of an innumerable army which was unable to pass, and he achieved other deeds such that were they recorded by another free and detached writer, instead of being related by himself with the modesty that befits a knight and a man who is his own chronicler, they would drive to oblivion the exploits of Hectors, Achilles, and Rolands.' (Part I, Chapter xxxii.)

Here, the priest who began preaching against the dancers ended in leading the dance. Little wonder that the Innkeeper flouts such achievements as stopping a mill-wheel with a finger and defending a bridge against an army and declares he prefers Don Felixmarte's exploits. And it must be owned that cutting five giants through the waist, all five at one stroke of the sword, riding a serpent of fire on a river, and suchlike deeds, are far more satisfactory than the Curate's 'historical' achievements, for while equally unbelievable they have the inestimable advantage of bursting open the bars of material reality and letting the wild imagination spread its mighty wings in freedom.

Thus we touch upon one of the main characteristics of Chivalry Books. It may be worth while defining them all. The first is the predominance of a feeling of love conceived as an attachment of an absolute and exacting quality, somewhat akin to religion, a passion for which men are ready to risk all manner of dangers and women to break all sorts of social bonds. The second is a freedom of imagination which does not stop even at the borders of common sense, but seeks satisfaction in the most extravagant fields of fancy. The third is the construction of plots as a kind of steeplechase which the hero and heroine must run, with the ultimate triumph of love and youth. These are the characteristics of melodrama, the literary *genus* most satisfying to the people. For the people, who do not care two straws for construction or consistency, who hold views on the unbelievable wisely free from undue attachment to the scientific tenets of the age, and whose main interests are instinctively on the side of youth and love, seek above all in literature a diversion from their own monotonous lives. The people have little power for fashioning their own lives, and rarely exercise their will on a great scale. It is therefore quite natural that they should find a singular pleasure in books that show omnipotent heroes before whose mighty will giants break in twain and castles crumble down. And, as a contrast with their own lives, made of ever-recurring obstacles, they cherish those stories where labours do have an end and everybody is at last happy. Books of Chivalry were therefore the melodrama of the age, and as that age had much less knowledge than ours, the field left to the imagination was much greater than nowadays. Cervantes thought he had killed Books of Chivalry with his *Don Quixote*, and it may be that he had contributed to their downfall. But in actual fact, Books of Chivalry died only in form (owing mainly to the fact that each age must re-create its own forms), while their spirit, which is the spirit of melodrama, did not die, and will not die save with the human race. It lives now in the film and the serial novel.

These are forms that appeal to the popular taste, but it does not necessarily follow that they are worthless. True they are condemned by the discerning and the critical. The intellect craves for order, a sequence, a purpose. It would reduce the world to a plan. But this craving of the intellect is not always satisfied by God's nature. Nature in fact is not unlike a Book of Chivalry in that it suggests an orgy of creative power, oblivious of all plan or object. Heard or unheard, the waves of the sea have always murmured and laboured, will always murmur and labour; seen or unseen, myriads of exquisite flowers put on their delicate silk and fade away; centuries of tender-coloured dawns blush and melt into days, whether man is asleep or awake; pine-woods bathe during ages in a sea of green coolness which no one has ever enjoyed; a butterfly is a lightning of beauty, a sunset lasts but a little longer than a sigh—and who can say that there is a plot in the story or that Nature aims at aught but pouring her creative power into the void of time? It is the critical mind that asks the question. But the people live and let live and the creative spirits do not ask. They know.

All this might be said *a priori*. But it is confirmed by the facts. Let us turn to that period roughly covering the sixteenth and seventeenth centuries, during which Books of Chivalry were read with delight and admiration all over the west of Europe. A striking resemblance will at once be noted between the historical facts regarding their popularity in Europe as recorded by modern research,[1] and the direct observations on their popularity in Spain which Cervantes embodied in his *Don Quixote*. In both cases three facts are prominent:

First: Chivalry Books are read by everybody. Don Quixote is not alone in his knowledge of them. Curate, barber, housekeeper and niece, innkeeper, wife and daughter, not forgetting Maritornes the servant, gentlemen met on the road, students, Duke and Duchess, and even the critical canon and the surly chaplain, all are familiar with Amadís and his progeny. So far, the novel. As for history, 'during the hundred years follow-

[1] Cf. *Spanish and Portuguese Romances of Chivalry*, by Henry Thomas, Cambridge University Press, 1920, pp. 147, 148.

ing the publication of *Amadís de Gaul*, some fifty new chivalresque romances appeared in Spain and Portugal. They were published at an average rate of almost one a year between 1508 and 1550; nine were added between 1550 and the year of the Armada; only three more came out before the publication of *Don Quixote*.[1] Add to this numerous translations and sentimental novels in which the chivalrous element is an important accessory. In Italy, France, Germany, Holland, and England Books of Chivalry attain equal popularity, a popularity, be it noted, which, while it extended to all classes of society, was particularly lively amongst women and the people.

Secondly : Men of intellectual distinction pronounce themselves against Chivalry Books. They voice the objections of classical taste as well as those of the moral and didactic mind against the licence of imagination and manners which Books of Chivalry reveal. The representatives of this class in *Don Quixote* are the Knight of the Green Coat, the Curate, the Chaplain, the Canon of Toledo—and Cervantes. In real life Luis Vives stands at the head of a legion of critics, literary and moral. And it is, by the way, worthy of notice that to his list of 'ungracious books', 'Amadise, Fluisande, Tirante, Turlane', Vives adds 'and Celestina, ye baude mother of noughtynes',[2] which shows how far removed from all creative sense Vives' criticism really was. In Italy critical disapproval is represented by

---

[1] Cf. *Spanish and Portuguese Romances of Chivalry*, by Henry Thomas, Cambridge University Press, 1920, pp. 147, 148.

[2] Quoted by Henry Thomas, p. 163, from the English translation of *De Institutione Fœminæ Christianæ*: Richard Hyrde, *The Instruction of a Christian Woman*, c. 1540, sig. E 4 recto–F 1 recto.

Girolamo Muzio (Henry Thomas, p. 197), whose
objections are an echo of that unconscious hanker-
ing of Cervantes after historical truth. In France we
find as we expected that Montaigne is against them.
In Germany Justus Lipsius is said to have condemned
Amadís, the best of them, as 'Ingeniosi nugatori proles,
pestilens liber' (Henry Thomas, p. 229), a judgement
similar to that which Dierick Coornhert will pass in
Holland. And in England, even if Sir Philip Sidney's
somewhat oblique slight on Amadís be left out of
account, the disapproving school had no less a chief
than Ben Jonson, the most classical mind in a Romantic
age.

Thirdly: Books of Chivalry are patronized by
princes and their courts, a few saints, and men rich in
the creative faculty. We know that Charles V (Henry
Thomas, p. 149), Francis I (ibid., p. 199), Louis XIV
(ibid., p. 221), William the Silent (ibid., p. 239), were
fond of them, and it is owing to princely patronage
that they were introduced into France, Italy, Holland,
and Germany. Everybody has read or heard that Saint
Teresa devoured them in her youth, and so did Saint
Ignatius Loyola even in his riper years. As for literary
creators favourable to the Romances, the list is long
and imposing. It begins with the great name of Lope de
Vega, who sums up all that precedes in a not inadequate
sentence:

'Many laugh at books of chivalry . . . and they are right
if they consider but the outward surface thereof . . . ; but
piercing the crust to the heart all the parts of philosophy
will be found therein; namely natural, rational and moral.'
(*Trecena parte de las Comedias*, Madrid, 1620. Quoted by
H. Thomas, loc. cit., p. 154.)

And along with the father of the Spanish theatre we find many of the great names of Europe—Torquato Tasso, Corneille, Madame de Sévigné, Goethe, Walter Scott, Dr. Johnson, Burke, and Keats, all of whom read or had read Books of Chivalry and confess to or declare various degrees of self-approval, self-excuse, or frank satisfaction.

There is little doubt that Cervantes, as a creative spirit, must be placed in this category. There is no lack of both direct and indirect evidence in support of this opinion. His incarnations in the novel—the Curate and the Canon of Toledo—reveal themselves in actual fact less averse to Chivalry Books than they had led us to expect. The Curate, in his scrutiny, exempts no less than four of them from destruction (*Amadís de Gaul, Belianís, Palmerín de Inglaterra,* and *Tirante el Blanco*), two of which he praises, somewhat whimsically in one case (*Tirante*) and extravagantly in the other (*Palmerin of England*). Moreover, this scene abundantly proves that Cervantes was extraordinarily well read in Chivalry Books and knew nearly all of them intimately and thoroughly which, to say the least, does not suggest an insurmountable dislike of them.

We are not therefore surprised when Cervantes, in the person of the Canon of Toledo, after delivering himself of all his critical objections against Chivalry Books, goes on to praise them in a passage which, however mixed in its literary criteria, is nevertheless a clear eulogy of them on the ground of the opportunities they offer to the creative spirit:

'Truly, Master Curate, in my opinion, these they call books of chivalry are very harmful to the community; and though, led by an idle and false taste, I have read the

c

beginning of almost all of those that have appeared in print, I never was able to read any one through to the end; for to me they all seem to be the same, little more, little less, and this one has in it nothing more than that one, and your one than the rest. It appears to me that this kind of writing and composition must be classed along with that of the fables which are called Milesian, which are extravagant stories aiming purely at pleasure and not at instruction, contrary to what is the case with the fables call Apologies, which seek both to instruct and to please. And though the main purpose of such books is to please, I fail to see how they can attain it, being filled with so many extravagancies, and so outrageous; for the pleasure which our soul conceives must rise from the beauty and harmony which it sees or beholds in the things which the sight or the imagination lay before it; and things which in themselves bear ugliness and disproportion cannot produce in us any pleasure whatever, for what beauty can there be, or what proportion of the parts to the whole and of the whole to the parts in a book or tale wherein a boy of sixteen years of age at one cut of his sword cleaves a giant as tall as a steeple through the middle as easily as if he were made of sugar paste? Or when they want to relate a battle to us, and after having stated that the enemy is one million strong, if only the hero of the book is against them, we are forced to understand that the said Knight attained victory by the mere virtue of his mighty arm? And what are we to say of the ease with which a queen or an heir-empress trustingly delivers herself into the hands of a knight errant and unknown? What mind, unless altogether barbarous and uncultivated, can find any pleasure in reading that a great tower, full of knights, cuts through the sea like a ship with a favourable wind, and to-night sees the sunset in Lombardy and to-morrow the dawn in the land of Prester John or in some other land never described by Ptolemy nor seen by Marco Polo? And if to this it were answered that the authors of such books compose them as men who avowedly write lies, and therefore are not bound to a nice respect for truth, I would retort that lies are the better as they more closely resemble truth, and the more pleasing as they contain more of the strange and the possible. Lying fables should match the understanding of their readers, being so contrived that reconciling their impossibilities, removing obstacles, keeping all minds in suspense, they may surprise, astonish, rejoice and entertain in such wise that pleasure and wonder may proceed apace; and all these things are impossible to him who strays from the verisimilitude of imitation—wherein lies the perfection of what is written. I have never seen a book of chivalry, the fable of which may be said to be an entire body with all its members and so that the middle corresponds to the beginning, and the end to the beginning· and the middle; but rather are they composed with so many members that their authors seem to aim at forming a chimera or a monster, and not a well-proportioned figure. Moreover, they are harsh in their style, incredible in their exploits, licentious in their love-affairs, inconsiderate in their courtesies, prolix in their battles, silly in their arguments, nonsensical in their travels, and finally altogether wanting in skill, and therefore worthy of being banished from the Christian Commonwealth as a useless breed.'

The priest listened to him with great attention, and took him to be a man of good understanding, and in the right in all he said; and therefore he told him, that, being of the same opinion, and bearing an old grudge to books of chivalry, he had burnt all those belonging to Don Quixote, which were not a few. Then he gave him an account of the scrutiny he had made, telling him which of them he had condemned to the fire, and which he had reprieved . . . (Part I, Chapter xlvii.)

On the strength of this passage and of all that precedes it in these pages, I venture to think that the real inception of *Don Quixote* must be found not in a desire to destroy, but in the ambition to emulate, the popularity of Amadís of Gaul and his race. Cervantes' first idea must have been that of writing a model Chivalry Book. Both this idea and the motive which inspired it are revealed to us by Curate and Canon, pursuing their conversation:

'It is as you say, sir,' quoth the Priest to the Canon; 'and for this reason, those who have hitherto composed such books are the more to blame, proceeding, as they do, without any regard to good sense, or art, or to those rules, by the observation of which they might become as famous in prose as the two princes of the Greek and Latin poetry are in verse.' 'I, at any rate,' replied the Canon, 'was once tempted to write a book of knight-errantry, in which I purposed to observe all the restrictions I have mentioned; and, to confess the truth, I had gone through above a hundred sheets of it. . . .' (Part I, Chapter xlviii.)

Here, I fancy, *Don Quixote* was born. From his first draft of a Book of Chivalry conceived in earnest, Cervantes must have been driven by his sense of humour to write a parody—a kind of literary activity much in vogue in his day. The rest was merely a pretext, more or less sincerely held, to explain away to others and to himself the apparent levity of the undertaking.

The Dualism of Don Quixote

OUR analysis of Cervantes' real attitude towards Chivalry Books has led us to suspect that he wrote *Don Quixote* under a complex system of motives, the least important of which probably was the one to which he gave most prominence throughout his work, i.e. the waging of a literary war against Romances of Chivalry. It is even suggested that this motive may not be a motive at all but a mere pretext to conciliate the serious-minded reader. This idea is strengthened by the fact that Cervantes was, as a writer, remarkably self-conscious. His work is full of remarks, suggestions, and expostulations for the benefit of the reader lest he be led astray by the critic, or of the critic lest he fail to see the difficulties of the task and the success of the author.

It will be remembered that Cervantes begins to entrench himself against unkind criticism from the very first page of his work, in his Letter of Dedication to the Duke of Béjar :

. . . So that under their shadow, though bereft of the precious ornament of elegance and learning that usually clothes works composed in the houses of discerning men, [Don Quixote] dare appear with self-assurance before the judgement of some who, unable to remain within the limits of their ignorance, are wont to condemn with more severity and less justice the works of others.

That these words, like many more in this Dedication, are copied from Herrera does not detract from the significance of their being put there by Cervantes.

This 'defensive' attitude against possible attacks

reappears in the Prologue, a light, ironical passage, yet revealing a self-critical preoccupation deeply set in the mind of the author. It is a preoccupation which is hardly ever absent from the book. Cervantes seems to seize every available opportunity to pass an opinion on his work. It is for this purpose that he puts his own *Galatea* among the books of Don Quixote's library:

'What is the next book?'
'The *Galatea* of Miguel de Cervantes,' replied the Barber.
'That Cervantes has been my intimate acquaintance these many years,' said the Curate, 'and I know he has been more conversant with misfortunes than with verse. His book is not altogether lacking in good invention; he aims at something yet achieves nothing; we must await the second part which he promises; perhaps he may then make amends and attain the mercy which we must now refuse him; and meanwhile, keep him a prisoner in your home.' (Part I, Chapter vi.)

He is no less quick to seize the next opportunity for self-criticism which the plot affords him, namely, the reading by the Curate of his novel *The Curious Impertinent*. When the reading is over, the Curate volunteers the following piece of criticism on the work.

'I like this novel well, yet after all I cannot bring myself to believe that it really happened; and if it be invention, it is ill invented, for no one could imagine that there could be a husband so foolish as to venture on so dangerous an experiment. Had the incident been related as happening to a gallant and his mistress, it might be accepted; but between husband and wife, there is something impossible in it. As for the way it is told it does not altogether displease me.' (Part I, Chapter xxxv.)

So far, Cervantes on himself when unprovoked. But, as the second part shows, and as his self-critical nature would lead us to anticipate, his self-consciousness was increased by outside criticism. Between the publication of the first and that of the second part, two sets of events reacted upon his mind. The first was the success of the book, which before the second part appeared went through numerous editions (seven within its first year). The second was a crop of criticism. Both these facts are reflected in the second part: his success gave him greater assurance, which can be discerned in the general tone of the work, its freer atmosphere and bolder invention, and which can actually be measured by comparing the two endings—the ending of the first part, modest, if only outwardly so ('forse altri canterà con miglior plettro')—that of the second part proud and haughty as befits a triumphant author:

And the most wise Cide Hamete, addressing himself to his pen, said: 'Here, O my slender quill, whether well or ill cut I know not, here, suspended by this wire, shalt thou hang upon this spit-rack, and live many long ages, if presumptuous or mischievous historians do not take thee down, to profane thee. But, before they offer to touch thee, give them this warning in the best manner thou canst:

> "Beware, beware, ye traitorlings,
> Let none, let none touch me,
> For this great work, oh good King,
> Was meant alone for me."

For me alone was Don Quixote born, and I for him; he knew how to act, and I how to write; we both alone are like two in one.' (Part II, Chapter lxxiv.)

In the inspiration of this second part, Cervantes' reaction against outward criticism is a powerful element. We shall see later on how skilfully he uses the success of the first part to develop and mature his characters, and particularly that of Sancho. Here we are purely concerned with the abundant evidence which it affords of Cervantes' self-consciousness and sensitiveness to criticism. Thus, in the third chapter—that in which Don Quixote, Sancho, and the Bachelor discuss the 'History of the Ingenious Hidalgo Don Quixote de la Mancha'—the Bachelor says:

'One of the faults people charge upon that history is, that the author has inserted in it a novel, entitled *The Curious Impertinent*; not that it is bad in itself, or ill-wrought, but that it is out of place and has nothing to do with the story of his worship Señor Don Quixote.' (Part II, Chapter iii.)

Here Cervantes does not see his way to answer the charge, but the memory of it brings it to his pen and he seeks relief in humour. The criticism, however, rankles in his heart, and he comes back to it, this time with a ready answer, at the beginning of Chapter xliv.

We are told that in the original of this history, it is said, Cide Hamete coming to write this chapter, the interpreter did not translate it, as he had written it: which was a kind of complaint the Moor made of himself, for having undertaken a history so dry, and so confined, as that of Don Quixote, thinking he must be always talking of him and Sancho, without daring to launch into digressions and episodes of more weight and entertainment. And he said, that to have his invention, his hand, and his pen always tied down to write upon one subject only, and to speak by the mouths of few characters, was an insupportable toil, and of no advantage to the author; and that, to avoid this inconvenience, he had, in the first part, made use of the artifice of introducing novels, such as that of *The Curious*

Impertinent, and that of *The Captive*; which are in a manner detached from the history; though most of what is related in that part are accidents which happened to Don Quixote himself, and could not be omitted. He also thought, as he tells us, that many readers, carried away by their attention to Don Quixote's exploits, could afford none to the novels, and would either run them over in haste, or with displeasure, not considering how fine and skilful they were in themselves, as would have been very evident, had they been published separately, without being tacked to the extravagances of Don Quixote, and the simplicities of Sancho. And therefore, in this second part, he would introduce no loose nor ill-connected novels; but only a few novel-like episodes, and such as flow naturally from such events as the truth offers; and even these, with great limitation, and in no more words than are sufficient to express them; and, since he restrains and confines himself within the narrow limits of the narration, though with ability, genius, and understanding, sufficient to treat of the whole universe, he desires his pains may not be undervalued, but that he may receive applause, not for what he writes, but for what he had omitted to write. (Part II, Chapter xliv.)

This passage gives the mood of his mind—the same mood which inspires the remarks of the Canon of Toledo and of the Curate in their critical conversations. It reveals the attitude of mind of an author whose creative impulse has to manifest itself against a heavy critical pressure from the environment of his age and country. The Spanish Golden Century—like its English counterpart, the Elizabethan Age—was in effect an epoch in which a splendid outburst of spontaneous and creative vitality coincided with an exceptional interest in and knowledge of classical and Italian models. The two events were so evenly timed together that we never think of one without the other; rather do we imagine them as two different aspects of the same fact, namely, the blossoming out of a brilliant artistic era. And so, no doubt, in a sense they are, for in actual fact life is always all-round and complete, and analysis is a thing of the mind. Yet it is, I believe, helpful to the better understanding of the spirit of Spain, of the Golden Century and of any one of the great names which flourished in it, particularly that of Cervantes, to realize that we are in the presence of two different phenomena, two different currents of spirit which happened to manifest themselves in the same men. The one is a purely vital and creative movement, which reveals the national soul seeking expression in spontaneous forms of art harmonious with her own genius. It is rooted in the genuine national forms, the most popular. It hails from the *Cantar de Myo Cid* and the *Mester de Juglaría*. It is linked with the Great Century by the free lances of poetry and creative invention, the great Archpriest of Hita, the Archpriest of Talavera, *Melibea* and the oral tradition of the ballads. It is romantic in inspiration, free and purely aesthetic in its outlook, and though tainted here and there with erudition in its actual creations, it owes nothing in its essence to Greece or Rome, still less to Italy or France. This movement grows apace with the development of the nation. It gives its first universal work under Ferdinand and Isabel. When, under the Austrian dynasty, Spain attains the first rank among the nations, it is only natural that the expression of the national soul should also attain its utmost splendour. True, the epoch of Philip IV was already well within the period of decadence. But the lapse of time was not more than was necessary for the national consciousness to realize

the fact and to pass from the mood of action which fills
the reign of Charles V to the mood of passion which
prevails under the Philips. Hence the magnificent
period which opens with Cervantes and closes with
Calderón. The Theatre, the Picaresque Novels, the
Romancero, the lyrical popular poetry (such poems
as *San Isidro* or *Los Pastores de Belén* of Lope), the
Letrillas of Góngora, and most of Saint Teresa and
Saint John of the Cross, all belong to this movement
of spontaneous national expression.

Alongside of it another movement advanced all
through the Middle Ages and matured at the same
time. It is the learned movement aiming at literature
written according to the accepted canon of scholarship.
It attracts to itself all the reflective, scholarly, and
didactic minds of the country, even those minds which,
in their moments of free and creative inspiration,
incarnate most felicitously the spontaneous spirit of
Spain. Its roots are in the *Mester de Clerecía*. Berceo
read French, and though he pretends to be 'popular' he
is a bookish author. The movement is academic, sometimes pedantic, and often didactic. Juan de Mena,
with his elaborate imitation of the Italians, Don Sem
Tob and his sententious proverbs, Micer Francisco
Imperial, the precursor of the Italian influence, Boscán,
all belong to it, along with nearly every second-rate
talent in the Peninsula. Santillana is frankly within
this movement in his Sonnets 'in the Italian fashion',
and in his *Comedieta de Ponza*, while he comes as near
to the popular and instinctive type as his aristocratic
mind allowed him to go in his delightful *Serranillas*.
The master of the movement is Garcilaso. As the
Golden Century draws near, the prestige of Italy,

renewing that of Rome and Greece, fosters in the cultivated mind of Spain a belief in that Trinity of Culture no less deep and sincere than that which then prevailed in the Holy Trinity of the Catholic Dogma. All the great names of the age—Fray Luis de León, Cervantes and Lope, Tirso and Calderón, Góngora and Quevedo—are learned men conversant with the Latin and Italian literatures, most of them also with the Greek and some even with the Hebrew language; all are classic in their conscious taste however romantic in their inspiration; all would, if the question were put to them, declare that the highest, nay the only models in literature and the arts are embodied in the works of the ancients; and all had a tendency to consider their own frequent departures from this sacred tradition either as money-making enterprises or as unimportant entertainments unworthy of literary consideration.

Such an age was bound to develop a strong taste for criticism as a sport, which does not necessarily mean a sound critical sense. And in actual fact it may be said that the period during which *Don Quixote* was written sees the high-water mark of literary activity in Spain. Under the two later Philips, the dominant sport in Madrid, Valencia, Valladolid, Seville, and every other important town was literature. A play, a book, was an event. How keen literary curiosity was is shown by the well-known fact that Lope de Vega passed a criticism (and an unfavourable one at that) on *Don Quixote* five months before its publication. The bitterness, the hard personal character which literary quarrels took in Madrid is proverbial. It will suffice to remind the reader of the exchange of amenities between Cervantes and Lope, of the relentless enmity between Góngora and

Lope, of the attacks on Alarcón and Quevedo, of the cabals against Calderón. It was in this over-sensitive world—brilliant, overcrowded with talent, seething with literary feuds—that Cervantes was launching his *Don Quixote*.

He was himself one of them. He had in him a royal measure of natural creative spirit; he had also a strong critical prepossession and rather fancied his scholarship, as witness the somewhat naïve remarks on translations which he puts in the mouth of Don Quixote when the Knight is visiting the Printing Works in Barcelona. He was endowed with at least the usual amount of sensitiveness to criticism; lastly he worked, as it were, under the eyes of a host of rivals eager to find a flaw. His natural self-consciousness was therefore exacerbated by the conditions under which he was working. And the point is important, for the main effect of self-consciousness in creative work is that it hinders the fusion of the elements which enter into the composition and prevents their blending into an harmonious unity.

Hence the complexity of *Don Quixote* as a literary work, for in it the diverse currents of influence which acted upon Cervantes at the time of writing appear flowing, as it were, side by side, and may be traced to their different sources. The most important of all, that which gives the work its immortal value, is the creative spirit of the people, as manifest in Cervantes' predecessors, and particularly in *La Celestina*. When Cervantes is in this vein he is at his best. Then his observation is so acute, his style so terse and clear, that the work is as reality itself to us. It is the vein of most of the dialogue-scenes between Don Quixote and Sancho. Cervantes is here the unprejudiced and spontaneous creator, the impartial observer and lover of men, whatever their condition, rank, virtue; the born writer who never sets down a word that is not living; the free artist who knows nothing but reality seen through emotion; the ideal poet, in whom the ever romantic imagination is instinctively guided and tempered by the ever classic common sense.

And now and then the learned gentleman with literary ambitions puts in a word. Then Cervantes tries to vie with the wits of Italy. He seeks the strange plot; he tries his hand at daintily twisted phrases; he courts the elusive metaphor. When this will-o'-the-wisp gets hold of his fancy it is the curious paradox of this most wonderful book that Cervantes seems to forget the very principles of classical order which he so admirably applies when under a spontaneous creative inspiration. Left to itself, his creative imagination, though romantic by nature, is classical in its sobriety, in the economy of its means, in the admirable restraint of its conception and expression. Hustled by his pseudo-classical conceits, this imagination which we saw so true and clear-sighted, seems to lose touch with the earth and indulge in extravagant and fanciful evolutions; matter and style become elaborate and needlessly complicated, and Cervantes is then as extravagantly romantic as he was severely classic when writing under the influence of his classical prepossessions.

We saw him pouring scorn on Feliciano de Silva's arabesques:

. . . but, among them all, none pleased him so much as those composed by the famous Feliciano de Silva: for the clarity of his prose, and those intricate speeches of his seemed to him exquisite; and especially when he came to peruse those love-praises and letters of challenge, wherein in several places he found written: 'The reason of the unreason which to my reason is meted out, in such wise my reason doth enfeeble that it is with good reason that I complain of your beauty.' And also when he read: '. . . the high heavens that of your divinity divinely fortify you with the stars, and make you meritorious of the merit which your greatness has merited . . .' (Part I, Chapter i.)

This verbal extravagance is by no means an exclusive feature of Chivalry Books as readers of Quevedo well know. Nor is it altogether without examples in England. Shakespeare himself indulged in it when writing his famous sonnet

Whoever hath her wish, thou hast thy 'Will'.

In writing his *Don Quixote*, Cervantes meant to break a lance in the cause of simplicity. And, in fact, his style is a model of simplicity . . . but only when he forgets all about it. As soon as he thinks of *writing*, of deliberately shining as a word artist, though he may not be extravagant he fails to attain to simplicity. The very first sentence of *The Curious Impertinent* (which pleased the Curate so much that he felt inclined to read the story through to his friends at the Inn) is a somewhat academic, almost pedantic sentence, ending with a wholly unnecessary inversion. The conversation between the Curate and the Canon of Toledo, in which Cervantes speaks as it were *ex cathedra*, often breaks into purely rhetorical chains of words, and rhetorical too must be declared the speech for the defence and for the prosecution which Ambrosio and Marcela pronounce over the body of the unhappy shepherd Grisostomo:

'Comest thou, peradventure, O fierce basilisk of these mountains, to see whether the wounds of this wretch, whom thy cruelty has deprived of life, will bleed afresh at thy appearance? or comest thou to triumph in the cruel exploits of thy disposition? or to behold from that eminence, like another pitiless Nero, the flames of burning Rome? or insolently to trample on this unhappy corpse, as did the ungrateful daughter on that of her father Tarquin? tell us quickly, what thou comest for, or what it is thou wouldst have: for since I know that Grisostomo, while living, never disobeyed thee, so much as in thought, I will take care that all those who called themselves his friends, shall obey thee, though he be dead.'

'I come not, O Ambrosio, for any of those purposes you have mentioned,' answered Marcela, 'but to vindicate myself, and to let it be known how unreasonable those are who blame me for their own sufferings, or for the death of Grisostomo: and therefore I beg of all here present, that they would hear me with attention; for I need not spend much time, nor use many words to convince persons of sense of the truth.' (Part I, Chapter xiv.)

But where this peculiar weakness of Cervantes is most apparent is in his occasional attempts at 'poetry'. Cervantes was—it is hardly necessary to say—rich in poetical feeling. When inspired by his creative imagination, he can reach poetical levels as high as that of the delightful scene where Teresa and Sanchica receive the Page who announces to them that Sancho is a governor. It is impossible to read that page without emotion. But Cervantes wanted to go farther than that. He wanted to prove himself a skilful versifier and an ingenious inventor of poetical conceits. And so he gives us Cardenio's song:

> What makes me languish and complain?
> > O 'tis disdain!
> What yet more fiercely tortures me?
> > 'Tis jealousy.
> How have I my patience lost?
> > By absence crost.
> Then hopes farewell, there's no relief;
> I sink beneath oppressing grief;
> Nor can a wretch without despair,
> Scorn, jealousy, and absence bear.
>
> What in my breast this anguish drove?
> > Intruding love.
> Who could such mighty ills create?
> > Blind fortune's hate.
> What cruel powers my fate approve?
> > The powers above.
> Then let me bear, and cease to moan;
> 'Tis glorious thus to be undone;
> When these invade, who dares oppose?
> Heaven, Love, and Fortune are my foes.
>
> Where shall I find a speedy cure?
> > Death is sure,
> No milder means to set me free?
> > Inconstancy.
> Can nothing else my pains assuage?
> > Distracting rage.
> What, die or change? Lucinda lose;
> O rather let me madness choose!
> But judge, ye gods, what we endure,
> When death or madness is a cure!
> > > (Part I, Chapter xvii.)

Now, if we remember that Cardenio's grief was such that it had reduced him to an almost savage life in the wilds of Sierra Morena, shall we not be justified in saying that this 'ovillejo', the most artificial of stanzas, is as extravagant a departure from simplicity as Silva's 'reason of the unreason'?

Thus Cervantes the author fell into the very faults derided in Books of Chivalry by Cervantes the critic. For indeed this seems to be a constant feature of his criticism that he is unable to generalize his views into a principle and that in practice he often presents, though in a slightly different form, the same defects which he condemns in theory. This is true of his matter no less than of his style. When criticizing the Books of Chivalry, he had so wittily ridiculed

> . . . Don Quixote de la Mancha, the light and mirror of Manchegan chivalry, and the first who in these calamitous times devoted himself to the labour and exertions of Knight-Errantry, to righting wrongs, rescuing widows and protecting maidens—those maidens who, with whip and palfrey, and with all their maidenhood about them, wondered from hill to hill, from dale to dale, so that unless a rogue or a villain in axe and helmet, or a boisterous giant ravished them, maidens there were in past ages who, after eighty years during which they never had slept under a roof, went to their grave as pure virgins as the mothers who bore them. (Part I, Chapter ix.)

Yet he made himself responsible for a good half-dozen of those wandering maidens whom he ridiculed when he met them with whip and palfrey in the hills and dales of Chivalry Books, but who seem quite acceptable to him when, clad in pastoral attire, they bewail their fate to the winds in the solitary haunts of Sierra Morena, or when, after many a perilous adventure, they are caught red-handed disguised as pirates in command of a Turkish brigantine. In these tales with which he sought to relieve the monotony of his main story, Cervantes claims back for himself a good share of the liberty which he denied the Books of Chivalry. Though he does not appeal to the marvellous, he does seek help in the unlikely—which is a kind of marvellous in its small way. Thus the two forces—unbridled imagination and weight of reality—which oppose each other in this book, have not yet achieved a state of balance. In his literary conception of the novel there is the same dualism which has been found in its two main characters—a dualism, I should add, just as complex and as full of inner influences and reflections. Now and then, realism prevails, and Cervantes is so conscientious as to take pains to explain the mechanism which underlies some of his ingeniously contrived adventures. (Altisidora's simulated death, or the Speaking Head in Don Antonio's house.) But how often, in true imitation of Don Quixote, does he gallop through the fields of imagination and lose sight of earth! Pastoral scenes in particular are his King Charles's head, just as Chivalry Books are Don Quixote's. For it seems indeed as if there were a subtle parallelism between the case of Don Quixote and that of his begetter—both men of sense, whose natural element is a simple acceptance of life and people as they are—and whose conduct is plain and quiet, yet both possessed of, obsessed by, an ambition, the one lured by the glory of arms and the other by the glory of letters into denying their own common sense and falling into extravagance.

There is indeed good ground for the view that much of the popularity which *Don Quixote* instantly gained was due precisely to the spirit of wild romance which it retained from the enchanted lands of chivalry and pastoral books whence it came.

> Not in entire forgetfulness
> And not in utter nakedness

but trailing clouds of fancy and romance.

Dorothea or Cleverness

DON QUIXOTE—like *Hamlet*, with which it is connected by not a few subtle sympathies and contrasts—is a world overflowing with vitality where characters, events, and stories are mingled and intertwined in generous abundance. We must leave till later the study of its central plot, which has a definite development, though—as in *Hamlet*—on the spiritual rather than the material plane. For on the material plane, the 'story' of *Don Quixote* has no plan other than the caprice of Rocinante. The itinerary of Don Quixote across the plains and hills of Spain threads together scenes and episodes with the purely accidental unity which a string lends a necklace. Yet the comparison is not accurate, for the episodes of *Don Quixote* are grafted on to the central story with varying degrees of intimacy. *The Curious Impertinent* is a frank intruder, smuggled into the work by a simple contrivance—the finding of a manuscript in a bag left by a visitor in the Inn where so many people come together at the close of Part I; and Cervantes is so badly afflicted with the tactlessness inherent in authors that, oblivious of the exhaustion so many travels, adventures, and emotions must have produced in his characters, he there and then forces them all to listen to his story before sending them to their well-earned beds. The captive's narrative is less of an intruder, since it refers to a character, however unimportant, in the main story itself. Doña Clara's episode is a shade more closely woven into the general story. As for the adventures of Cardenio and Dorothea, they can hardly be considered mere episodes since these two persons play important roles in the life of our hero.

The extraordinary wealth of narrative material heaped together by Cervantes in the closing chapters of Part I has been variously interpreted even in his lifetime. His own opinion on the matter may be gathered by reading—mostly between the lines—certain passages in Chapters xl and xlv. Cervantes seeks variety for fear that a plot limited to two characters may lead to monotony. But measured by this standard, Part II is obviously inferior to Part I, a fact which has strengthened the preference for Part I that a number of critics have been rash enough to evince. Nevertheless this sudden boiling over of stories and episodes at the end of Part I may be a sign not of creative power but rather of the reverse, for its suggests a certain hesitation in the author as to the central plot. Cervantes seems here to let go the thread of his main story and to lose sight of the development and destiny of his two immortal characters. The rapid succession of episodes which suddenly break into the main narrative precisely towards the end of the work—for this was then obviously the end of his work and Part II was not conceived till much later—is less the rich reward of fresh inspiration than the padding of a tired author who disperses in minor tasks an effort no longer sufficient for his main creation. It will be remembered that this is also the moment when Cervantes delivers his critical lectures in the form of dialogues between the Canon of Toledo and the Curate in pages which, though full of interest for the scholar, are a dead weight on the work considered in its aesthetic purity. We are then in the presence of a double parenthesis

—creative and critical—which suggests a certain lack of attention on the part of Cervantes to his main creation.

The very reverse will be observed in the second part. Cervantes has regained full control over his central theme, and his creative impulse is not to waver again in its easy yet sure progress to the beautiful and moving end. The reader feels the vital force which makes the novel proceed along its magnificent main road without straying into side ways and episodes. But Cervantes-the-conscious feels the sacrifice which Cervantes-the-subconscious exacts from him and we hear the sighs of his literary vanity in the curious beginning of Chapter xliv. (See passage quoted, p. 66.)

We cannot withhold our sympathy for so ingenious an inventor of tales and plots. Every step of Don Quixote's progress is a pretext or an opportunity for his wonderful fertility to create a plot, an episode, a biographical sketch. The very letter which Teresa Panza sends her illustrious husband, risen to the rank of governor of an island, gives Cervantes scope for two impromptu short stories:

. . . The news of this town is, that the Berrueca is about marrying her daughter to a sorry painter, who is come to this town to paint whatever should offer. The magistrates ordered him to paint the king's arms over the gate of the town-house: he demanded two ducats: they paid him beforehand: he worked eight days, at the end of which he had made nothing of it, and said he could not hit upon painting such trumpery. He returned the money, and, for all that, he marries under the title of a good workman. It is true, he has already quitted the pencil, and taken the spade, and goes to the field like a gentleman. Pedro de Lobo's son has taken orders, and shaven his crown, in order to be a priest. Minguilla, Mingo Silvato's grand-daughter, has heard of it, and is suing him upon a promise of marriage; evil tongues do not stick to say she is with child by him : but he denies it with both hands.

The adventure of the galley slaves provides an opportunity for the string of biographies which reveal the keen psychological insight of the author. This adventure is significant in that it illustrates Cervantes' gift as an inventor of stories. He is led to story-writing by his vanity, a desire to prove his ability to weave plots and intrigues—an attitude which is self-conscious and literary; yet what he really proves is a much deeper and richer gift, a creative inspiration born of a curious mind, a keen penetration and a profound sense of human values. Cervantes is the model of the dominant tendency of all Spanish art, i.e. its interest in men, seen, not as symbols or types, but as definite individuals, complex and concrete, who refuse to be classed into regular series.

This sense of the human, which is at the core of his creative power, is the peculiar virtue which gives so much life to every one of the characters in the book. For instance that delightful giant Pandafilando of the Cross Sight whom Dorothea, as Princess Micomicona, improvises in passing in order to make her story acceptable to Don Quixote. A few touches suffice the sprightly lady for the giant to stand before us on the stage, not a romantic monster but a human being, albeit extravagant :

A monstrous giant, lord of a great island, almost bordering upon our kingdom, called Pandafilando of the Cross Sight (for it is averred, that though his eyes stand right, and in their proper place, he always looks askew as if he squinted; and this he does out of pure malignity, to scare and frighten those he looks at : . . .) (Part I, Chapter xxx.)

For Pandafilando is a creation not merely of Cervantes but of Dorothea. The tone in which it is conceived is the same wherewith the 'discreet' young woman neatly interprets the comedy contrived by the Curate and the Barber in order to bring Don Quixote back home. A well-meaning comedy, to be sure, but still somewhat uncouth and awkward, lacking the last touch of art which puts the bloom of reality over the face of imitation. That last touch Dorothea gives it when she joins in the plot, bringing to it a gracefulness and a humour which are not only feminine but motherly as well, for Pandafilando is a nursery villain. The reader is delighted to find that Dorothea is ready to lend a helping hand to the Curate and the Barber in their charitable scheme and to take on the difficult role of Princess Micomicona. She is the ideal woman for it —above all clever, in my opinion the cleverest person in the whole Quixotian world. She speaks with remarkable ease and command of words, an important feature in which both speed and accuracy suggest an exceptional quickness of observation and comprehension and an intellect used to the handling of ideas.

With his usual acuity, Cervantes has noted this natural eloquence of his clever damsel, her felicitous choice of words and even a certain pleasure in finishing off neatly rounded sentences, a feature which often goes with a tendency to play upon words. Dorothea, even when engaged in the narrative of her misfortunes, sees her way to present her listeners with no fewer than three puns. The passages are not always translated so as to preserve them. The following are mere endeavours to remain faithful to the text even in this, in my opinion significant, feature of Dorothea's way of speaking:

'. . . but to cut short the countless account of my misfortunes . . .' ('. . . mas por acabar presto con el cuento [que no le tiene] de mis desdichas . . .')

This first pun, it must be owned, is rather Cervantian than Dorothean. Cervantes uses it also in one of Cardenio's speeches.

'. . . I found neither cliff nor ravine to make my master pass from grief to grave . . .' ('. . . no hallé derrumbadero ni barranco de donde despeñar y despenar al amo . . .')
'. . . I say then that I returned to my cover and to try to discover where . . .' ('digo, pues, que me torné a emboscar y a buscar donde . . .') (Chapter xxviii.)

Lest the reader might doubt Dorothea's fondness for word-play and think the above examples due to mere chance, more appear farther on. Thus in Chapter xxxvi Dorothea says to Don Fernando:

'In fine, Sir, what I say last of all is, that . . . if you value at all that for which you undervalue me . . .' ('En fin, señor, lo que últimamente te digo es que . . . si ya es que tu precias de aquello por que me desprecias . . .')

In Chapter xliii, hearing a somewhat involved confession from Doña Clara, she expostulates:

'You speak in such a manner, Señora Clara, that I cannot understand you: declare yourself more fully and tell me . . .' ('Habláis de modo, señora Clara, que no puedo entenderos: *declaraos* más y decidme . . .')

But her masterpiece in this art is the play of words which enables her to convey the most difficult and delicate fact in her story:

'. . . and my maid having left the room, I ceased to be one myself . . .' ('. . . y con volverse a salir del aposento mi doncella yo dejé de serlo . . .')

In this verbal complacency, as of a person who hears herself speak, Cervantes makes us feel the chief feature of Dorothea, her intellectual character, her cleverness. Men of action, usually slow of thought and tardy of speech, often admire clever people, mistaking for real wisdom what is but an image of wisdom mirrored by the intellect and language. Dorothea's father, the rich farmer Clenardo, had entrusted his daughter with the management of his estate. And yet he probably knew the Spanish dictum that fools say foolish things and clever people do them, a profound observation which reminds us that in action cleverness is rather a hindrance than a help, since the mind acts before the courts of conscience as counsel for desire, and the cleverer the counsel the more likely the victory of the party.

Such sober thoughts are apt to occur to the reader as he enjoys the admirable narrative in which the sprightly damsel sums up her misfortunes. It is an analytical narrative, as was to be expected of so keen a mind, and it reveals that instinctive art for marshalling facts which is a natural gift of clever people. Throughout the story we feel intellectual activity constantly awake which, not content with stating events, delves into motives, guessing, analysing, supposing them, and which tends to sum up dialogues in the form of arguments. For the young woman never loses her lucidity, and even at the moment of dramatic surprise when Don Fernando breaks into her bedroom at midnight, while the bold lover holds her in his arms, she argues for and against in her active head with the detachment of a lawyer. Don Fernando of course abstains from arguments, lavishing instead the usual tokens of love—tears, promises, and solemn oaths. He is not clever but he knows his business. For while Dorothea might have saved her honour had he followed her on to her dialectical field, she was a defenceless prey on the field of instincts and emotions where he kept her. While Don Fernando piles oaths upon promises, Dorothea turns her own weapons against herself:

'Upon that occasion I briefly reasoned thus with my-self: Well: I shall not be the first, who, by the way of marriage, has risen from a low to a high condition, nor will Don Fernando be the first, whom beauty, or rather blind affection, has induced to take a wife beneath his quality. Since then I neither make a new world, nor a new custom, sure I may be allowed to accept this honour, which fortune throws in my way; for though the inclina-tion he shows for me, should last no longer in this world than the satisfaction of his desire, yet, in the sight of God, I shall be his wife. Besides, should I reject him with dis-dain, I see him prepared to set aside all sense of duty, and to have recourse to violence: and so I shall remain dis-honoured, and without excuse, when I am censured by those, who do not know how innocently I came into this strait. For what reasons can be sufficient to persuade my parents, and others, that this gentleman got into my apartment without my consent?'[1]

An admirable interpretation of the psychology of cleverness. The maid 'ceases to be one' and remains

---

[1] There is another instance in the Spanish text of Dorothea's ten-dency to word-play: 'sin disculpa de la culpa'.

'I know not whether sad or gay' without strength to scold her servant for having concealed Don Fernando in her room, since she cannot make up her mind whether what has happened was good or ill. Such is, in fact, the fate of the clever, for when their instinct fails to upset the balance of logic, their mind remains vacillating on the edge of two equal arguments.

Events, however, came to break her suspense, and the news of Don Fernando's wedding thrust her again into action in a manner which reveals yet another of her characteristics—impulsiveness. It is a feature often found along with cleverness. One might even look upon cleverness as a kind of mental impulsiveness, whence the insecurity and the incoherence wherewith the clever pay the devil for their brilliancy. Cleverness, moreover, often leads the will to a cul-de-sac, since all the avenues of action can be equally lit up by the mind; so that in the end the clever have to act impulsively, thus adding to their natural impulsiveness an acquired impulsiveness due to the failure of their minds to supply a clear ruling. Dorothea is no exception, as may be seen in her own account of her reaction on learning of Don Fernando's marriage:

'This sad news soon reached my ears; and my heart, instead of being chilled at hearing it, was so incensed and inflamed with rage and anger, that I could scarce forbear running out into the streets, crying out and publishing aloud, how basely and treacherously I had been used. But this fury was moderated for the present by a resolution I took, and executed that very night; which was, to put myself into this garb, which was given me by one of those, who, in farmers' houses, are called swains, one who was my father's servant, to whom I discovered my whole misfortune, and begged of him to accompany me to the city, where I was informed my enemy then was. He, finding me bent upon my design, after he had condemned the rashness of my undertaking, and blamed my resolution, offered himself to bear me company, as he expressed it, to the end of the world. I immediately put up, in a pillow-case, a woman's dress, with some jewels and money, to provide against whatever might happen: and in the dead of that very night, without letting my treacherous maid into the secret, I left the house, accompanied only by my servant, and by many imaginations, and took the way that led to the town on foot, the desire of getting thither adding wings to my flight, that, if I could not prevent what I concluded was already done, I might at least demand of Don Fernando, with what heart he had done it.'

This impulsive action leads Dorothea through various incidents to the recesses of Sierra Morena, a refuge no doubt chosen by Cervantes with the delicate intention of giving us the pleasure of meeting and knowing her. For it is delightful to hear her talk. She is an admirable narrator and controls words and arguments with so much assurance that one gains the impression that her misfortunes have not struck her soul very deep. And such is generally the case with clever people, for they are better able than others to defend their inner self against the thrust of life. Our impression is strengthened when—to our moderate surprise—the much tried young woman offers herself to take on the role of Micomicona; for Dorothea does not suggest herself out of charity alone but also for the fun of it. She is sure of her ability:

... and they might leave it to her to perform what was necessary for carrying on their design, she having read many books of chivalry, and being well acquainted with the style the distressed damsels were wont to use, when they begged their boons of the knights-errant.

Events were to prove her right in trusting to her imagination, well stocked as it was with Chivalry Books (which by the way cannot have been so objectionable since they contributed to form such delightful persons). In this world of free creation Dorothea feels in her element. Stimulated by the expectant audience and even somewhat excited and carried away by the vitality of her imagination, she gives her whole self to her task with a most attractive generosity. Hence the charm of her impersonation of Princess Micomicona, due to the spontaneous and natural way wherewith she enters into the role with her youthful assurance bordering on forwardness yet within the bounds of modesty, her sense, her discretion, and exquisite humour. The touch of forwardness is admirably suggested. It appears in the warmth of improvisation, when the faked princess declares that her father, Tinacrio the Wise, had prophesied that one, Don Azote or Don Gigote, who was to save the kingdom of Micomicón from Pandafilando's tyranny

. . . was to be tall and thin-visaged, and that on his right side under the left shoulder, or thereabouts, he was to have a grey mole with hairs like bristles.'

Later she offers her person to her liberator in words which subtly suggest a certain licentiousness of imagination :

'. . . who, moreover, left it written . . . that, if this knight of the prophecy, after he has cut off the giant's head, should have a mind to marry me, I should immediately submit to be his lawful wife, without any discussion, and give him possession of my kingdom, together with my person.'

Again during the discussion on Chivalry Books with the Innkeeper's family she puts the Innkeeper's daughter out of countenance with a delightful question which no one but Dorothea could think of asking:

'I listen too; and truly, though I do not understand it, I take some pleasure in hearing it: but I have no relish for those blows and slashes, which please my father so much; what I chiefly like is the complaints the knights make when they are absent from their mistresses; and really, sometimes, they make me weep, out of the pity I have for them.'

'So you would not fail to relieve them, young maid,' said Dorothea, 'if they wept for you?'

Finally, when the plot Cardenio–Luscinda–Don Fernando–Dorothea has been brought to its happy conclusion, and Sancho reveals to his master that he has noticed strange liberties passing between Don Fernando and Princess Micomicona:

'Nothing of all this, as I am a sinner to God,' answered Sancho, 'only that I am sure and positively certain, that this lady, who calls herself queen of the great kingdom of Micomicón, is no more a queen than my mother; for, were she what she pretends to be, she would not be nuzzling at every turn, and in every corner, with somebody that is in the company.'

Dorothea herself saves the situation. Too frank to lie, too loyal to consent that Sancho should be punished for no fault of his own, the quick young woman finds a solution worthy of her talent and adaptability:

'Be not offended, good Sir Knight of the Sorrowful Figure, at the follies your good squire has uttered: for, perhaps, he has not said them without some ground; nor can it be suspected, considering his good understanding and Christian conscience, that he would slander, or bear false witness against anybody: and therefore we must believe, without all doubt, as you yourself say, Sir Knight, that since all things in this castle fall out in the way of enchantment, perhaps, I say, Sancho, by means of the same diabolical illusion, may have seen what he says he saw, so much to the prejudice of my honour.'

But when her natural light shines brightest is in the scene which crowns the whole adventure, her unexpected meeting with Don Fernando and Luscinda (Part I, Chapter xxxvi). On the strength of a number of verbal blemishes Señor Rodríguez Marín has pointed out that this whole chapter is written rather carelessly, 'todo él escrito harto desaliñadamente'. The opinion of Spain's chief 'Cervantist' may be fully confirmed by observing the inconsistencies of fact which abound in its pages. The reader of *Don Quixote* will remember that while Dorothea and Cardenio are in the Inn with their new acquaintances, the Curate and the Barber, Don Quixote and Sancho, 'a fine company of guests' arrive at the Inn, all wearing black masks; chief among the new-comers are a lady 'looking ill and without force' and a gentleman whom every one respects and obeys. Cardenio hides himself in Don Quixote's room while Dorothea veils her face. At this point, Cervantes begins to build up a jigsaw puzzle of recognitions between his several characters. Cardenio and Luscinda (who is the lady looking ill and without force) are the first to recognize each other on hearing each other's voices. Luscinda thereupon feels much agitated and on Don Fernando endeavouring to hold her, both let drop their masks. Then Dorothea, who recognizes Don Fernando's face though she had not recognized his voice, faints. The Curate unveils her face to throw water on it, and Don Fernando recognizes her. Cardenio

D

who—though an expert in Luscinda's voice—thinks Dorothea's 'oh' has been uttered by Luscinda, rushes out of his hiding-place and meets Don Fernando still holding Luscinda in his arms; and then Cervantes adds: 'All were silent and all were looking: Dorothea at Don Fernando, Don Fernando at Cardenio, Cardenio at Luscinda, and Luscinda at Cardenio.'

The situation is admirably conceived in harmony with the respective characters. But let it be noticed that Dorothea has come to and that both Don Fernando and Luscinda have recognized Cardenio. And yet, the next paragraph but one, coming as it does after a long speech of Luscinda, begins thus: 'Meanwhile Dorothea had come to herself . . .' and farther on, when Don Fernando, conquered by Dorothea's entreaties, lets Luscinda go, Cervantes says: '. . . Cardenio who happened to be close by, for he was behind Don Fernando so as not to be recognized by him . . .' Let us grant that Cardenio having recognized Don Fernando, imagines that Don Fernando has not recognized him. But what of the next paragraph? We saw how Cardenio and Luscinda had recognized each other when hearing each other's voices, and later how they had remained looking at one another. We heard two speeches after this, one by Luscinda, begging Don Fernando to let her go to 'the wall of which I am the ivy' and still Cervantes writes: 'Hearing these words Luscinda set eyes on Cardenio and having begun to recognize him by his voice and making sure afterwards that it was he by looking at him . . .' These are abundant proofs of negligence, not merely of style but as to the very facts of the narrative. Yet they do but enhance the value of the chapter as a significant example of marvellous accuracy in character-drawing even under this distracted attention towards externals. We catch a glimpse of that unswerving subconscious attention which remains attached to the characters despite the wanderings of the conscious intellect. With all its negligence in style and story, this is one of the chapters in *Don Quixote* in which Cervantes' psychological insight is at its best, and there is not one word, look, gesture in it which does not fit perfectly with the character to which it is attributed. Indispensable to the knowledge of Cardenio, this page brings out in all its clearness the figure of Dorothea. She abstains from reproaching Don Fernando for his behaviour. Her aim is to recover her honour by making of this haughty nobleman her husband. Her means must be to reconquer that love which she once lost through a too liberal gift of herself. And knowing him to be proud she stoops to conquer. Far from throwing his treason in his face and claiming her rights, the shrewd young woman reminds him that she is 'that humble farmer's daughter whom your kindness or your pleasure wished to raise to the level of calling herself yours'. She declares herself ready to be his slave if he will not take her as a wife, and, with a touch of astuteness, adds that if he persists in his perjury his own conscience will come to spoil his future pleasures. Small wonder then that Don Fernando yields to the entreaties of so beautiful and intelligent a woman. Always respectful towards the great, Cervantes lavished grace and beauty on this delicately drawn figure whom he was to make the wife of a duke. When he speaks of her there is a special tenderness in his words. Dorothea was his favourite daughter.

Cardenio or Cowardice

THERE is perhaps no scene in the whole of *Don Quixote* more delicately prepared than that of the meeting between the Knight of the Sorrowful Figure and the ragged One of the Sorry Figure, Cardenio, whose furious and fitful madness contrasts with the continuous and consistent madness of Don Quixote. The technique of Cervantes, skilful rather than convincing when the author is intent on what he is doing (see for example *The Curious Impertinent*), is unfailing when he lets himself be carried away by his creative inspiration. Observe the contrast in the ways in which Dorothea and Cardenio are presented. Dorothea appears in a pastoral scene. One scene is enough to reveal her completely, as she is: quick of speech, open, impulsive, intelligent and sprightly. Cardenio, on the contrary, is a mystery gradually revealed in a series of sudden appearances cut short by intervals of absence and obscurity. His history is as ragged as his figure. He enters the story through the incident of a lost portmanteau, 'some heavy bundle that lay upon the ground' which Don Quixote tried to lift with the point of his spear. The portmanteau reveals that its owner is rich—the gold crowns which Sancho appropriates—and in love—the little notebook which Don Quixote scrutinizes. From the artificial and involved style of the sonnet and the letter which Don Quixote reads aloud, we might infer other traits of Cardenio's character; but we prefer to attribute them to Cervantes' literary foible and pass on. Meanwhile the outline of the character emerges gradually out of conversation and conjectures between Don Quixote and Sancho, becoming a little more concrete on the discovery of the dead mule half eaten by dogs and pecked by jackdaws and later by the conversation with the goatherd who appears over the top of the mountain. Whistlings, shouts, cries, leaps, crags, all the unsteadiness and restlessness of the approaching character are already there in the technique of his presentation. This agitation still pervades the narrative of the goatherd who describes the character in a series of dramatic encounters and dramatic disappearances. And at last the person himself appears down a deep cleft of the Sierra 'muttering to himself something, which could not be understood, though one were near him, much less at a distance'. Cardenio reaches the group and greets them in a hoarse discordant voice. And then there occurs that wonderful scene in which the two madmen look long into each other's eyes, each trying to find in the other the reason of his un-reason. This contrast between the clear and instantaneous appearance of Dorothea and the confused, tortuous, gradual, and disconnected appearance of Cardenio is an admirable image of their respective characters. Dorothea is cleverness, Cardenio cowardice.

On the basis of cowardice Cardenio's character is built up with marvellous penetration. First, observe the courtesy and good manners which mark his normal state: 'When the youth came up to them he saluted them . . . with much civility.' The goatherd had already drawn this trait of his character. 'He saluted us courteously.' '. . . he was a very comely and graceful youth, and by his courteous behaviour and civil discourse, showed himself to be well born, and a court-like person.' This courtesy at times reaches humility. 'He thanked us for our offers, begged pardon for the violences passed, and promised from thenceforth to ask it for God's sake . . .', said the goatherd. And Cardenio himself, before beginning his narrative: 'If you have anything to give me to eat, give it me, for God's sake, and when I have eaten, I will do all you command me, in requital for the good wishes you have expressed toward me.' Still more subtly observed appears another tendency very much in the character of the coward, a kind of intellectual obsequiousness, which shows itself in ready acquiescence with other people's opinions. Two successive instances may be found in a fairly short fragment of Cardenio's story:

'He [the father of Luscinda] answered me, that he thanked me for the inclination I showed to honour him and myself in my proposed alliance with his family; but that, my father being alive, it belonged more properly to him to make this demand; for, without his full consent and approbation, Luscinda was not a woman to be taken or given by stealth. I returned him thanks for his kind intention, thinking there was reason in what he said, and that my father would come into it as soon as I should break it to him; and in this mind I went on the instant to acquaint my father with my desires; and upon entering the room where he was, I found him with a letter open in his hand, which he gave me before I spoke a word, saying to me: "By this letter you will see, Cardenio, the inclination Duke Ricardo has to do you service." This Duke Ricardo, gentlemen, as you cannot but know, is a grandee of Spain, whose estate lies in the best part of Andalucia. I took and read the letter, which was so extremely kind, that I myself judged it would be wrong in my father not to comply with what he requested in it; which was, that he would send me presently to him.'

Cowardice, while it occasionally manifests itself as fear of concrete dangers, in reality dominates the soul of the coward in the form of a diffuse fear. Thus Cardenio:

'In a word, I told him, that I durst not venture to speak to my father about it, as well for that drawback as for many others, which disheartened me, I knew not why; only I presaged, that my desires were never to take effect.'

Here we have, well defined, the diffuse, unreasoned, almost superstitious fear; fear of a mythical enemy, the condensation of all past defeats on the field of action. The pressure of this diffuse fear makes the vitality of the coward flow back again within him, and so Cervantes notes in Cardenio the strong tendency to introspection. He becomes speculative by a natural law since, in the field of speculation, the will is exercised only on oneself, not on others. At every step Cardenio evinces this tendency to introspection which, although intellectual in essence, differs from the cleverness of Dorothea precisely in its reflective character which contrasts so greatly with the mental impulsiveness characteristic of the clever. Cervantes has admirably rendered this delicate shade that separates the two characters on their intellectual side. Observe how they tell their respective stories. What in Dorothea is a spontaneous ebullition of ideas, words, and arguments, felicity of expression, and even verbal pleasure, in Cardenio is a slow and reasoned exposition broken by questions, distinctions, excuses, and imprecations. And while Dorothea, though quick and instinctive, is clear, Cardenio, though reflective and argumentative, is confused. He advances in one direction, loses himself, stops, comes back upon his track, returns to his original idea, and ends by falling into greater confusion. In this way there is reflected in his story the mental disorder to which his irresolution leads him, and that necessity to find arguments which is second nature in the coward. For, in the coward, introspection adds an acquired and, so to speak, secondary irresolution to his primary or innate one.

This is the weak man of whom Destiny, in the person of Don Fernando, makes a plaything. His whole history is one continuous giving of himself up to events. The path of the weak is paved with unfulfilled decisions. Cardenio gives up his at the slightest obstacle that presents itself. On merely finding his father with a letter in his hand—a letter moreover which affects his own destiny and that of the woman he loves—he renounces his intention of begging him to ask for Luscinda's hand. He determines to inform Duke Ricardo of Don Fernando's adventure with the rich farmer's daughter (who turns out to be Dorothea), and a transparent stratagem of the young man is enough to put him off until his plan becomes ineffective. He guesses the danger in Don Fernando but, with that lack of intellectual courage which in cowards is the fear, not of the conclusion, but of the action which must follow it, he does not dare to recognize it. From this it follows that once the occasion for action is over he recovers his insight:

'True it is (I confess it now) that though I knew what just grounds Don Fernando had to commend Luscinda, I was grieved to hear those commendations from his mouth, and I began to fear and with reason to suspect him.'

He receives the letter Luscinda sends him in the pages of *Amadís de Gaul*, and is moved to ask her in marriage; but this resolution takes him no further than to say to Don Fernando:

'I told Don Fernando what Luscinda's father expected; which was, that my father should propose the match; but that I durst not mention it to him, lest he should not come into it: not because he was unacquainted with the circumstances, goodness, virtue, and beauty of Luscinda, and that she had qualities sufficient to adorn any other family of Spain whatever; but because I understood by him, that he was desirous I should not marry soon, but wait until we should see what Duke Ricardo would do for me.'

Don Fernando gets him away from the place on a poor pretext and, in spite of Luscinda's tears, he goes, unhappy man, 'sad and pensive, his soul filled with imaginations and suspicions', and when Don Fernando's elder brother keeps him back against his will, Cardenio himself reveals his fatal irresolution in a phrase most felicitous in its incoherence:

'This injunction put me into such a condition, that I could not presently think of obeying it, it seeming to me to be impossible to bear life under an absence of so many days from Luscinda, especially considering I had left her in so much sorrow, as I have already told you. Nevertheless I did obey, like a good servant, though I found it was likely to be at the expense of my health.'

Despairing news from Luscinda shakes him out of his irresolution. He returns on wings, filled with anger against Don Fernando; but he goes to see Luscinda, not the traitor. He finds her in her bridal dress, beneath which she has a dagger hidden so that, if necessary, she can fly from the arms of the betrayer to the arms of death. And stimulated by such decision Cardenio holds forth with manly words:

'Let your actions, madam, make good your words; if you carry a dagger to secure your honour, I carry a sword to defend you, or kill myself, if fortune proves adverse to us.'

Words which his own actions belied. He enters by stealth the house where the marriage and his sacrifice are to be consummated. Unseen he hides in the embrasure of a window and at the critical moment, while anxiously awaiting the *Yes* or *No* which will fall from the lips of Luscinda he reaches the height of his irresolution:

'O! that I had dared to venture out then, and to have cried aloud, "Ah! Luscinda, Luscinda! take heed what you do; consider what you owe me; behold, you are mine, and cannot be another's. Take notice, that your saying *Yes*, and the putting an end to my life, will both happen in the same moment. Ah, traitor Don Fernando! ravisher of my glory, death of my life! what is it you would have? what is it you pretend to? consider, you cannot, as a Christian, arrive at the end of your desires; for Luscinda is my wife, and I am her husband." Ah, fool that I am! now that I am absent, and at a distance from the danger, I am saying I ought to have done what I did not do. Now that I have suffered myself to be robbed of my soul's treasure, I am cursing the thief on whom I might have revenged myself, if I had had as much heart to do it as I have now to complain. In short, since I was then a coward and a fool, no wonder if I die now ashamed, repentant, and mad.'

Luscinda's *Yes*, her swoon, the general hubbub, and the flight of Cardenio are perhaps the best part of the story. This flight deserves to be compared with that of Dorothea. This is how he himself describes it:

'Perceiving the whole house in a consternation, I ventured out, not caring whether I was seen or not; and with a determined resolution, if seen, to act so desperate a part, that all the world should have known the just indignation of my breast, by the chastisement of the false Don Fernando, and of the fickle, swooning traitress. But my fate, which has doubtless reserved me for greater evils, if greater can possibly be, ordained that at that juncture I had the use of my understanding, which has since failed me; and so, without thinking to take revenge on my greatest enemies (which might very easily have been done, when they thought so little of me), I resolved to take it on myself, and to execute on my own person that punishment which they deserved; and perhaps with greater rigour than I should have done on them, even in taking away their lives; for a sudden death soon puts one out of pain; but that which is prolonged by tortures, is always killing, without putting an end to life. In a word, I got out of the house, and went to the place where I had left the mule: I got it saddled and without taking any leave, I mounted, and rode out of the town, not daring, like another Lot, to look behind me; and, when I found myself in the field alone, and covered by the darkness of the night, and the silence thereof inviting me to complain, without regard or fear of being heard or known, I gave a loose to my voice, and untied my tongue, in a thousand exclamations on Luscinda and Don Fernando, as if that had been satisfaction for the wrong they had done me.'

How different the flight of Dorothea. What, in Cardenio, is flight from the duty of action, abandoning the field of battle and the ensuing despair and flight from himself is, in Dorothea, a wave of impulse which bears her along to seek the traitor, this very Don Fernando from whom the betrayed Cardenio is fleeing:

'. . . and [I] took the way . . ., the desire of getting thither adding wings to my flight, that, if I could not prevent what I concluded was already done, I might at least demand of Don Fernando, with what heart he had done it.'

The rest of the adventure is but an adapting of herself to the new and difficult circumstances which this unconsidered act of hers creates for her: whereas, in Cardenio, we see the passions kindled in his soul rising higher and higher by what we should today perhaps call an involution of his anger suppressed by his cowardice.

Cardenio himself in an admirable phrase describes this psychological phenomenon of which he is the victim:

'I was totally confounded, and thought myself abandoned of heaven, and become an enemy to the earth that sustained me, the air denying me breath for my sighs, and the water moisture for my tears: the fire alone was so increased in me, that I was all inflamed with rage and jealousy.'

A phrase built on the four elements: earth, air, water, fire, but not for that less graphic and profound. Nature, and in particular human nature, is based on earth, air, water, and fire. And, in describing his state of mind after the catastrophe of his life as a predominance of the fire element, Cardenio makes us feel the terrible transition from his sanity to his insanity. Indignation, suppressed by cowardice, turns against the coward and burns up his reason. The courteous, obsequious, and even humble Cardenio becomes obsessed by violence. The goatherd has already described this feature in his earlier appearances:

'. . . until, some days after, he issued out upon one of our shepherds, and, without saying a word, came up to him, and gave him several cuffs and kicks, and immediately went to our sumpter-ass, which he plundered of all the bread and cheese she carried; and, this done, he fled again to the rocks with wonderful swiftness.'

As if to define the contrast between Cardenio sane and Cardenio insane Cervantes makes the goatherd say farther on:

'. . . for, when the mad fit is upon him, though the shepherds freely offer it him, he will not take it without coming to blows for it; but when he is in his senses, he asks for it for God's sake, with courtesy and civility, and is very thankful for it, not without shedding tears.'

Here is a concrete case of Cervantean creation in which the character is built up in accordance with the newest psychology . . . and the oldest common sense. The stored-up fury which burns in Cardenio and breaks out without motive whenever the Censor, reason, is absent, is nothing else than the exasperation of the will, which we saw so weak just when it was most essential that it should be strong. Cervantes carries his character along through his mad attacks until he brings him out again into a state of sanity no less meek and feeble than the initial one. His convalescence begins when he hears from the lips of Dorothea that, when Luscinda fainted, a paper had been found in her bosom in which she 'declared that she could not be wife to Don Fernando because she was already Cardenio's . . .' and that she had given her consent to Don Fernando, merely in obedience to her parents. These words make hope and courage spring up again in Cardenio and he offers himself to Dorothea in terms which Feliciano de Silva himself would not have repudiated:

'For I swear to you upon the faith of a gentleman and a Christian, not to forsake you, until I see you in possession of Don Fernando, and, if I cannot by fair means persuade him to acknowledge what he owes to you, then to take the liberty, allowed me as a gentleman, of challenging him justly with my sword for the reason of the unreason he has done you; forgetting the injuries done to myself, vengeance for which I leave to heaven, that I may the sooner redress yours on earth.'

In spite of this, when destiny brings all the protagonists of the affair together at the Inn, Cardenio, who begins by hiding in Don Quixote's room, keeps throughout the whole scene his same irresolute attitude. Cervantes carries his observation of the character to a point of pitiless and cruel precision. The reader will remember that, from the opening of the scene, Don Fernando holds Luscinda closely in his arms while first she and then Dorothea beg him to let her go to Cardenio. Then Cardenio. . . . What is he doing all this time? Watch him. . . . Dorothea ceases to plead whereupon Don Fernando:

. . . opened his arms, and, leaving Luscinda free, said: 'You have conquered, fair Dorothea, you have conquered; for there is no withstanding so many united truths.'
Luscinda was so faint, when Don Fernando let her go, that she was just falling to the ground. But Cardenio, who was near her, and had placed himself behind Don Fernando, that he might not know him, now laying aside all fear, and ready for all risks, ran to support Luscinda . . .

As if repenting of his cruelty, Cervantes allows his character a sudden impulse of valour. When, with Luscinda in his arms, he sees Don Fernando making as if to revenge himself on his rival, while Dorothea intercedes:

. . . Cardenio . . . kept his eyes fixed on Don Fernando, with a resolution, if he saw him make any motion towards assaulting him, to endeavour to defend himself, and also to act offensively as well as he could, against all who should take part against him, though it should cost him his life.

And Don Fernando again overpowered, more, to tell the truth, by the entreaties of the beautiful Dorothea than by the attitude of his rival, everything ends in a scene which only the customs of the time and the humble character of Cardenio himself explain :

. . . and then Cardenio and Luscinda went and kneeled before Don Fernando, thanking him for the favour he had done them, in such terms of respect, that Don Fernando knew not what to answer; and so he raised them up, and embraced them with much courtesy and many demonstrations of affection.

The Real Don Quixote

DON QUIXOTE, Sancho, Don Juan, Hamlet, and Faust are the five great men created by man. Resembling in this the great men made directly by the Creator, their forms have been covered in each generation by a new over-growth of legends, opinions, interpretations, and symbols. Such is the privilege of those living beings of art who by sheer vitality impress their personality on the collective mind of mankind.

In Faust the tendency to germinate ideas is already part of the character as it leaves the mind of Goethe (perhaps even the mind of Marlowe). Goethe is a peculiar poet, very German in his intellectualism, in his interest in culture and philosophy which set him in a noble and exalted atmosphere of concepts and symbols even when he is expressing himself as a creative artist. Of such concepts and symbols is made the figure of Faust. No wonder that every generation of readers adds its own 'ideosphere' (to coin a word) to the already rich intellectual atmosphere in which the character was conceived.

There is nothing of this in Shakespeare, pure poet, 'feeler' rather than thinker, as Unamuno would say, whose thought runs, in its vitality, like a sap or like blood, through the vigorous body of his poetry. But Hamlet stimulates our intellectual activity by the feeling of silence and void which the mystery of his character conveys. A marvellous creation! Vague and unexplained to the mind, real and concrete to the instinct, known before he is understood as are persons and their affairs in life, Hamlet is a concavity, a human void that the mind strives to fill with its own thoughts and interpretations. Hence the harvest of ideas about Hamlet which every generation throws into the abyss of his obsessing personality.

Don Juan attracts the critics for a number of reasons such as the variety of his type and evolution from Tirso's great but unequal comedy to Zorrilla's preposterous but spirited one; his obviously representative quality as a hero of tyrannical love, the modern variety of inexorable Aphrodite; and, last but not least, the natural tendency in every writer to enrich the Don-Juan psychology with his own donjuanesque experiences.

But in Don Quixote and Sancho, the harvest of ideas, interpretations, and symbols which grow and accumulate round them is due solely to the depth of their souls, to the wealth of the human subsoil which Cervantes explored in them and to that subtle rhythm of the twofold adventure which seizes and impresses the imagination at the very outset with its apparent simplicity and later conquers the mind with its amazing complexity.

In this way the original figures of Don Quixote and Sancho have been buried under a growth of ideas and symbols, some absurd, others profound and penetrating, most of them inspired by a parallelism which does not exist in the book and is the result simply of a false and superficial antithesis between the Knight and the Squire. The Don Quixote–Sancho pair are interpreted as a 'contrast' and their characteristics converted into two series of antagonistic values. From Don Quixote is drawn the series 'valour-faith-idealism-utopia-liberalism-progress', while the Sancho series is made to develop in the opposite direction as 'cowardice-scepticism-realism-practical-sense-reaction'. But even putting aside these overgrowths of the semi-scholarly imagination, so fertile and so rich in error, and limiting the field to the more philosophical and deeply thought out criticism, one is perhaps at liberty to think that, in the very wealth of their spirit, which stimulates the thought of commentators, Cervantes' two characters tend to become obscure and to disappear beneath the intellectual luxuriance which they have been feeding with their own vitality.

Through this tanglewood of symbol and inter-pretations let us return to Don Quixote and Sancho as Cervantes saw them.

The case of Don Quixote is one of self-delusion. We know the main facts about what we might call his 'normal' character, for Cervantes took care to scatter them about, particularly in the opening chapters. He is 'about fifty, of a tough constitution, lean-bodied, thin-faced, an early riser and a lover of hunting'. He is unmarried, and Cervantes took special pains to let us know why: for when he comes to the choosing of a Lady, in whose honour to fight, we are told that 'in a village not close to his own there lived a good-looking country-lass, with whom he had once been in love, though it is believed she never knew of it or noticed it'. So, our good hidalgo is a shy man in matters of love, and therefore apt to idealize. He has indeed not a few of the features of the dreamer and idealist. Thus we learn that he was often idle: 'when he happened to have nothing to do, which was almost the whole year round . . .' and as is usually the case with idle dreamers, he read. That he read Books of Chivalry is no wonder, for apart from the fact that most books were Books of

Chivalry, what better reading was there to fill in the idle moments of an idealistic dreamer? Moreover, he was fond of the theatre as he tells us himself: '. . . Ever since I was a boy I loved the "Mask" and my eyes longed after the players . . .' (Part II, Chapter xi). His courtesy is a by-word and so is his generosity. His good sense, a little higher and finer than common sense, yet wholly within reason, though less obvious, is sure in all that does not touch Knight-Errantry. His kind and fraternal soul was enriched by a religion sincere in its faith, reverent in its form, and reserved in its manifestations. Thus putting two and two together we find what sort of a man is Alonso Quijano—a fine type of Spanish gentleman, a friend to solitude, given to swift pacing, nay galloping, over the fields of imagination and worthy in his earnestness and good faith to overstep the borderline of sanity on the side which touches the divine.

THE INNER ENEMY OF DON QUIXOTE

By dint of much reading and little sleep Alonso Quijano, giving himself over to his dreamings and imaginings, passes the threshold of reason. He becomes possessed of a delusion which, formed within the dark chambers of his own brain, he knows to be vain and deceptive, but, quickened by the breath of his imagination, worthy of loyalty and sacrifice. And to this delusion Alonso Quijano, in the process of becoming Don Quixote, will faithfully hold until the sleep from which he wakens to sanity, not long before the sleep from which he wakens to eternal life. The growth of this delusion, Don Quixote's jealous guard over it against all outer attack (from the world) or inner attack (from his own soul), the gradual wearing down of it by relentless reality, and its final vanishing—along with the ebb and flow it produces in the brave knight's spirits—that, so far as Don Quixote is concerned, is the substance of the novel.

The first shock with reality comes when Don Quixote tries the strength of his makeshift beaver with his sword. For, like a good idealist, he thought he could make a beaver out of pasteboard as he had made a Knight-Errant out of Alonso Quijano and a Lady Dulcinea out of a country wench. The beaver broke at the first slash of a real sword and Don Quixote never forgot the lesson. When he had repaired the damage and even strengthened it with 'iron bars inside', he prudently refrained from putting it to the proof again, entrusting the strength to his own firm decision to hold it a good sound beaver. From this moment Don Quixote will never again trust reality and will avoid putting his beliefs to the test whenever he scents the slightest danger of being belied by facts. Thus, after the battle with the flocks of sheep :

'You must know, Sancho, that it is a very easy matter for such [enchanters] to make us seem what they please; and this malignant one, who persecutes me, envious of the glory he saw I was likely to acquire in this battle, has transformed the hostile squadrons into flocks of sheep. Now, Sancho, do one thing, for my sake, to undeceive yourself, and see the truth of what I tell you : get upon your ass, and follow them fair and softly, and you will find that, when they are got a little farther off, they will return to their first form, and, ceasing to be sheep, will become men, as straight as men can be, as I described them at first . . . But do not go now; for I want your help and assistance. . . .' (Part i, Chapter xviii.)

And again when the battle with the wine-skins is over, and he appears before Dorothea and entreats her to trust in him, the knight carefully avoids carrying his assertions to the extreme limit of what he has imposed upon himself as true:

'. . . he would have found at every turn, how other knights, of a great deal less fame than myself, have achieved matters much more difficult, it being no such mighty business to kill a pitiful giant, be he never so arrogant; for not many hours are past since I had a bout with one myself, and—I say no more, lest I should be thought to lie: but time, the revealer of all things, will tell it, when we least think of it.' (Part I, Chapter xxxviii.)

And observe how, when the Innkeeper gives him the lie somewhat roughly: 'You have been fighting with two wine-skins, not with a giant,' Don Quixote does not reply, taking refuge in silent contempt from the dangers of an unequal argument.

Thus protected his self-delusion grew. At the beginning it was secret and timid. On his first sally the brand new Knight steals out by the door of the backyard 'without giving anyone a hint of his intention' and 'without being seen'. And to these details, which reveal how insecure his new faith is, Cervantes adds others no less significant: Don Quixote feels 'great joy and exultation on seeing how easily he had begun to put his scheme into practice', a shrewd sidelight on his self-distrust. For it is one of the most admirable features in Cervantes' handling of the character of Don Quixote that, even in his madness, his reason is not made to die out altogether but is as it were asleep, lightly asleep, with intervals of lucidity which make it emerge now and then to the surface.

Don Quixote has not reached a clear consciousness of his personality. His delusion still lacks form. In this unfinished stage two incertitudes are inextricably mingled: one proceeding from the still fluid soul of the character; the other from the soul of his creator. Señor Menéndez Pidal has illustrated, as he so well knows how to do, the vagueness of Cervantes in this first outline of his hero. (*Un aspecto en la elaboración del 'Quijote'*. Ateneo Científico, Literario y Artístico de Madrid, 1920.) The adventure with the merchants from Toledo must be considered a deflexion or twist in the development of the type which, as Señor Menéndez Pidal has shown, is due to the attraction of a foreign body, namely the *Entremés de los Romances*, a parody of the *Romancero* which Cervantes must have known. Under the influence of this work Cervantes makes Don Quixote wander, imagining himself Baldwin in the Ballad of the *Marquis of Mantua* and further on the Moor Abencerraje relating his love affairs to the *Alcaide* of Antequera. In both of these delusions the Don Quixote of this adventure is merely imitating Bartolo in the *Entremés*. The vacillation here is rather in the mind of the author than in that of the hero. But in these early beginnings of the character, when it has as yet hardly issued from the folds of its creator's mind, Cervantes' vacillation adapts its rhythm unconsciously to the vacillation of his hero. And had not the Spanish scholar elucidated this detail, what henceforward must be considered an error—since, strictly speaking, this curious deviation of the character is an aesthetic error—might have seemed an interesting phase in the evolution of Don Quixote.

From this moment on, the character remains faithful

to his own line of evolution. But how subtly observed are the movements of his spirit round this main chimera. In his first adventures there is an underlying lack of self-assurance in the Knight. The Innkeeper who gives him the accolade allows himself not only jests, which the poor madman does not notice because they are beneath his level, but to give advice and instruction which Don Quixote accepts with the humility of a novice. Soon, however, we begin to notice a certain vigour in his voice, which suggests if not assurance, at least a determination to impose his faith upon his own and other people's doubts. Thus, when the giants turn out to be mere windmills, Don Quixote explains the transfiguration in a phrase which brings into admirable relief the way in which the will imposes as truth what to the intellect is mere conjecture:

'Peace, friend Sancho,' answered Don Quixote; 'for matters of war are, of all others, most subject to continual mutations. Moreover, I think, *and it is most certainly so*, that the sage Friston who stole away my chamber and books, has turned these giants into windmills, on purpose to deprive me of the glory of vanquishing them . . .' (Part I, Chapter viii.)

And again, on the following day, when leading up to the adventure of the Biscayan:

'Either I am deceived, or this is like to prove the most famous adventure that ever was seen; for those black bulks that appear yonder must be, *and without doubt are* enchanters, who are carrying away some princess, whom they have stolen, in that coach . . .' (Part I, Chapter viii.)

Thus Don Quixote seizes reality by the neck before it has time to give him the lie, with the swiftness which is the form that fear takes in the man of action. For, mad as he was, he was the father of his own delusion, and could not kill within him the voice that told him it was all vain imagination. Hence his eagerness to seize upon everything likely to confirm his belief. Listen to his words of profound satisfaction to Sancho, after the victory over the Biscayan:

'But tell me, on your life, have you ever seen a more valorous knight than I, upon the whole face of the known earth? Have you read in story of any other, who has, or ever had, more bravery in assailing, more breath in holding out, more dexterity in wounding, or more address in giving a fall?' (Part I, Chapter x.)

Words not of vanity but of relief from his doubt, of modesty at bottom, as Cervantes subtly points out at the end of the same chapter when he says:

. . . but, if Sancho was grieved that they could not reach some habitation, his master was so much rejoiced to lie in the open air, making account that every time this befell him, he was doing an act possessive, or such an act as gave a fresh evidence of his title to chivalry.

This undercurrent of doubt, this inner enemy, the most formidable of all he ever fought, which in the end overpowered him, taking from him the desire to live, will accompany him throughout his whole heroic life. A great deal of his wonderful energy is to waste itself in that inner and silent struggle which comes to the surface now and then in moments of distress. Thus when Sancho, who has been present at the denouement of the episode of Dorothea, reveals to him the news that the Princess Micomicona is just an ordinary lady and when Dorothea, intent on continuing the hoax, denies the report, Don Quixote admonishes Sancho in words of great harshness which show his deep perturbation:

'I tell thee now, little Sancho, that thou art the greatest little rascal in all Spain: tell me, thief, vagabond; didst thou not tell me just now, that this princess was transformed into a damsel called Dorothea; and that the head, which, as I take it, I lopped off from a giant, was the whore that bore thee; with other absurdities, which put me into the greatest confusion I ever was in all the days of my life?' (Part I, Chapter xxxvii.)

And much later when he is received by the ducal household with all the ceremony with which he had read knights-errant were received in the Castles of Fancy, Cervantes says:

. . . and this was the first day that he was thoroughly convinced of his being a true knight-errant, and not an imaginary one . . . (Part II, Chapter xxxi.)

THE MYTH OF DULCINEA

Contriver of his own glory, Don Quixote, then, carried within his own soul his most dread enemy: the consciousness that it was all illusion. His attitude towards this enemy is the same as towards those from outside, one of valour and fortitude. And so we see him fighting every attack which menaces the safety of his inner fortress.

Remember the disastrous ending of the adventure with the galley-slaves. Don Quixote, reluctantly following Sancho's advice, agrees to hide in the Sierra Morena out of reach of the Holy Brotherhood. But scarcely has he yielded to the voice of prudence proceeding from the mouth of Sancho than he hears in his innermost being the voice of doubt, his enemy within.

And immediately he sets to work to drown it under energetic and persistent protests:

'. . . but upon this one condition, that neither living nor dying, you shall ever tell anybody that I retired and withdrew myself from this peril out of fear, but that I did it out of mere compliance with your entreaties: for if you say otherwise, you will lie in so doing; and from this time to that, and from that time to this, I give you the lie, and I tell you, you lie and will lie every time you say or think it: and reply no more; for the bare thought of withdrawing and retreating from any danger, and especially from this, which seems to carry some shade or no shade of fear with it, makes me, that I now stand prepared to abide here, and expect alone, not only that holy brotherhood you talk of and fear, but the brothers of the twelve tribes of Israel, and the seven Maccabees and Castor and Pollux, and even all the brothers and brotherhoods that are in the world.' (Part I, Chapter xxiii.)

The same state of intimate alarm inspires his action at the beginning of Part I, Chapter xliv. He has spent a good part of the night hanging from the window of the barn; for the hand which he gallantly offered to the 'Lord of the Castle's' daughter had been basely tied to the bars of the barn window by the infamous servant Maritornes. And in this situation he was surprised by the four horsemen who arrived at the Inn in search of the fugitive Don Luis. When finally the early morning bustle wakens Maritornes and she unties the good knight who has been left hanging in the air by an unexpected movement of Rocinante, Don Quixote forgets the pain in his hand in order to minister to the pain in his heart and:

. . . raising himself upon his feet, mounted Rocinante, braced his target, couched his lance, and taking a good compass about the field, came up at a half-gallop, saying: 'Whoever shall dare to affirm, that I was fairly enchanted, provided my sovereign lady the princess Micomicona gives me leave, I say, he lies, and I challenge and defy him to single combat.'

Here we have a vivid instance of Don Quixote's sensitiveness to the movements of his own moods and of his swift response in the way he proceeds to restore his prestige in his own eyes before the ravages caused by the humiliations of infamous reality have gone too deep.

By will and stern watchfulness he is enabled so to strengthen his faith that he can feed his delusion from his delusion itself. This is the height of his splendour. In this period Don Quixote lives on his own faith. And a strong faith it had to be to weather that return journey which ends the first part of this most cruel book. A prisoner in a cage, Don Quixote thinks himself enchanted, and to Sancho's only too sound arguments against such an easy and comfortable explanation of his situation, Don Quixote answers triumphantly:

'. . . and [I] know of myself, that no force but that which is supernatural could be sufficient to imprison me . . .' (Part I, Chapter xlviii.)

Yet even here Cervantes mixes with a master hand the subtle essences of doubt and faith. And so Don Quixote, in the following chapter, says:

'. . . I know or hold that I am enchanted; and that is sufficient for the discharge of my conscience, which would be heavily burdened if I thought I was not enchanted, and should suffer myself to lie in this cage like a lazy coward, defrauding the necessitous and oppressed of that succour I might have afforded them . . .' (Part I, Chapter xliv.)

And farther on, to the goatherd, who has pummelled him and is holding him on the ground:

'Brother devil (for it is impossible you should be anything else since you have had the valour and strength to subdue mine) . . .' (Part i, Chapter lii.)

This blend of self-delusion and self-knowledge, and the complexity it involves, is what makes the character so human and vivid. Cervantes handles it so skilfully that the unity and consistency of the stout-hearted Knight is never spoilt. There is a significant passage in the book which brings this out. It is when Don Quixote, on sending Sancho with a letter for Dulcinea del Toboso, reveals to him that the lady of his thoughts is no other than Aldonza Lorenzo, the daughter of Lorenzo Corchuelo and Aldonza Nogales. On hearing this Sancho is startled and breaks forth into one of his inimitable outbursts of astonishment, wonder, satire, and vituperation, driving his master to the defensive-offensive position which obliges him to reveal the secret of his imagination.

An admirable page even in a book so full of admirable pages, not only for its substance but for its tone and mood. Don Quixote reveals to Sancho that the true Dulcinea, whosoever the person representing her in real life may be, is a creation of his own brain and therefore perfect. But this revelation which between equals would have been easy, becomes painful owing to the chasm separating the planes of their respective philosophies: the conscious idealism of the master, the instinctive realism of the servant. It falls to the master to try to bring them together and interpret them, first because he is the superior in station and then because it is he, after all, who is on the defensive. And so, gallantly, as becomes a knight-errant, Don Quixote adventures without fear on the plane of Sancho's realism. But Cervantes skilfully draws the good Knight's awkwardness when riding so far below his own level. The story of the free beautiful widow in love with a young lay brother, which Don Quixote produces to make Sancho understand his own attitude to Dulcinea-Aldonza, rings false in its vulgarity on lips like his accustomed to delicacy of thought. The idealist endeavouring to meet the realist miscalculates his distance and falls into cynicism. (We would mention here, though this will be more fully discussed later, that Don Quixote misjudges his Squire and this causes him also to exaggerate the difference in level between the two.) Once this episode is over the Knight regains his moral authority and gives vent to the shrewd remark :

'. . . that in this though he be condemned by the ignorant, he will not be punished by the wise . . .'

after which quick sally into the sunny fields of reason he returns to the shadows of madness and writes that delightful letter to Dulcinea-Aldonza in the true style of Amadís.

This chapter makes clear to us the value which Don Quixote attaches to Dulcinea. For him Dulcinea is an incarnation of all the values (as we should say today) for which a knight can and should sacrifice himself. Dulcinea is, in a word, Glory. Now Glory is an elastic conception ranging from vainglory to Eternal Glory; but, within this vast compass, each knight chooses his Dulcinea according to the loftiness and purity of his ambition. Don Quixote, in creating in his imagination a perfect Dulcinea worthy of his sacrifice, did not fail by a long way to include in his myth the glory of living in the memory of men. His name, his fame, his honour are precious things to him. Cervantes in the very first chapter says so:

... he thought it expedient and necessary, as well for the advancement of his own reputation, as for the public good, that he should commence knight-errant ...

a sentence in which the advancement of his honour is put before the service of the commonwealth. But the Knight himself is no less clear when, after the memorable adventure of the fulling-mills, he rebukes Sancho for his unseemly laughter:

'I do not deny but that what has befallen to us is fit to be laughed at, but not fit to be told; for all persons are not discreet enough to know how to take things by the right handle.' (Part I, Chapter xx.)

We must draw attention already then to his preoccupation with his good name. Up till now it has been a secondary trait in Don Quixote's character; later it will be seen to develop and add still further complications to his already complex personality.

The Real Sancho

WORKS of genius attract all mankind; the high, the low, and the average. In which they differ from works of mere talent which only interest the average. This is an advantage in one way but a disadvantage in another. For in every work of art there is collaboration between the artist and the public, so that works of genius tend inevitably to become the work of all. As a work of art becomes popular it undergoes a certain deformation due mostly to simplification. It has been claimed that the chief merit of *Don Quixote* lay in the extreme simplicity of the characters. This may indeed *seem* to be the case, but it is not so. *Don Quixote* owes its popularity, not its *merit*, to the fact that the characters are capable of simplification and once simplified still continue to be of the greatest interest. It is like a symphony the melody of which runs in one's head and so becomes popular, but this does not prevent it from possessing at the same time a rich harmonic texture, closely and subtly woven.

Such is *Don Quixote*. Superficial tradition has reduced its marvellous psychological fabric to a line of simplest melody. Don Quixote, a valiant knight and idealist : Sancho, a matter-of-fact and cowardly rustic. What tradition does not see is that this design which, on a first impression, is based on contrast, resolves itself into a complicated and delicate parallel, the development of which is one ofthe subtle achievements of this book of genius. *Sancho is, up to a point, a transposition of Don Quixote in a different key.* Such cases of parallelism are seldom lacking in great works of art. Like Laertes and Fortinbras to Hamlet, or Gloucester to King Lear, Sancho is a parallel to Don Quixote, bringing out the main figure and enriching the design of the whole.

Both are men endowed with abundant gifts of reason, intellectual in Don Quixote, empirical in Sancho, who at a certain moment become possessed of a self-delusion which unbalances their mind and life. But while in Don Quixote this self-delusion gathers round a nucleus of glory symbolized in Dulcinea, in Sancho it gradually takes form round a kernel of material ambition, symbolized in an island. The Curate's words were not empty:

'. . . we shall see the drift of this machine of absurdities, of such a knight and such a squire, who, one would think, were cast in the same mould; and indeed the madness of the master, without the follies of the man, would not be worth a farthing.'

For indeed Don Quixote and Sancho are true brothers and their maker planned them after the same pattern.

WAS SANCHO PANZA A COWARD?

This fraternity between Don Quixote and Sancho, which Cervantes puts so plainly into the mouth of the Curate, has been not a little obscured by the over-simplification which, as we have said, both characters have undergone. Thus, for example, the antithesis required that, as Don Quixote is valiant, Sancho must be a coward, and behold Sancho converted into a symbol and personification of cowardice. The book does actually present a case of cowardice admirably conceived and drawn, but such is the power of the simplifying prejudice from which readers of *Don Quixote* have suffered that, overlooking cowardice in Cardenio where it is the axis and centre of his character, they attribute it to Sancho in whose character it does not exist, at any rate as a permanent or essential feature.

Let us recall some of the episodes of his life. His fight with the goatherd when Cardenio's narrative is interrupted by a fit of madness, a scene to which we shall have to return later; his gallant bearing as Governor of the island of Barataria, not to speak of his firm attitude towards Doctor Pedro Reico de Tirteafuera whose head he threatens to break with a chair, and towards the wag of Miguel Turra whom he dismisses firmly but with a moderation which in itself is a true sign of manliness. Lastly, the unhappy scene where the squire lays hands on his master, when the latter, impatient to release his Dulcinea, tries to hasten matters by taking on himself the flogging of Sancho.

In spite of these and other scenes of a similar nature, Sancho holds, in literature, the reputation of being a coward. This error is in part due to Don Quixote himself, who misses no opportunity of accusing his squire of lack of courage. But it would be too credulous and, moreover, unjust to Sancho, to take literally all that Don Quixote says of his faithful servant. Don Quixote was a knight-errant with small faith in his own credentials. The strengthening of his faith in his own knight-errantry had come to be a vital instinct for him like that of self-preservation. He must needs be pardoned then if, to satisfy this instinct, he sacrifices everything, even the good name of his squire. His frequent allusions to Sancho's

E

cowardice are so many more indirect assertions of his own valour.

The impatient way in which Sancho at times receives them ought to put us on our guard. For example, the ending of Chapter xx, Part ii, when, with a touch of irony and superiority, Don Quixote says:

'. . . but I can in no wise understand, nor comprehend, how, since the fear of God is the beginning of wisdom, you who are more afraid of a lizard than of Him, should be so knowing.'

And Sancho answers:

'Good your worship, judge of your own chivalries, and meddle not with judging of other men's fears or valours; for perhaps I am as pretty a fearer of God as any of my neighbours . . .'

This answer reveals some resentment in Sancho and, if it be true that the superior tone of his master was irritating, it is no less true that Sancho himself now and again gave ground for interested or superficial observers to think they saw in him flashes of cowardice. As this point touches the honour of one of the two greatest men that Spain has produced, it is worth while to attempt to elucidate it a little carefully. Let us observe then, to begin with, that Sancho, far from being a coward, shows himself a virile type of man whose courage has a primitive, animal, almost bestial quality. Cervantes has brought out this vital impulse of his hero in scenes which leave the matter in no doubt. Let us return for instance to the scene of the goatherd mentioned in Part i, Chapter xxiv. Cardenio has broken off short in his story, provoked by an interruption from Don Quixote into a fit of madness which ends in a violent attack on the author of this slight incident:

'Sancho Panza, seeing his master handled in this manner, attacked the madman with his clenched fist,' by no means the deed of a coward, 'and the Ragged Knight received him in such sort, that with one blow he laid him along at his feet; and presently, getting upon him, he pounded his ribs, much to his own heart's content.' A similar fate befell the goatherd who ran to Sancho's defence. But the comic moment of the scene occurred when, once the madman had gone 'with gentle calm', 'leaving them all pounded and beaten', Sancho felt the rage of defeat boil within him. And this Sancho, a 'coward' according to his calumniators :

. . . got up in a rage, to find himself so roughly handled, and so undeservedly withal, and was for taking his revenge on the goatherd, telling him he was in fault for not having given them warning, that this man had his mad fits; for had they known as much, they should have been aware, and upon their guard. The goatherd answered, that he had already given them notice of it, and that, if he had not heard it, the fault was none of his. Sancho Panza replied, and the goatherd rejoined; and the replies and rejoinders ended in taking one another by the beard, and cuffing one another so, that, if Don Quixote had not made peace between them, they would have beat one another to pieces.

Said Sancho, wrestling with the goatherd :

'Let me alone, Sir Knight of the Sorrowful Figure; for, this fellow being a countryman, like myself, and not dubbed a knight, I may very safely revenge myself on him for the injury he has done me, by fighting with him hand to hand, like an honest man.'

Over this boiling animal courage is the lid of sound common sense which makes him not combative but pacific. Fighting in itself is not pleasant. Sancho is ready to fight, but only when there is a reason, i.e. a cause for it. As opposed to his master who fights for sport and as part of his calling as knight, Sancho will fight only when he sees something to be gained by it, a purse, his life, or whatever it may be, since his reasons for fighting increase as he grows in moral stature. To this is due his attitude on not a few of the occasions on which his master mistakes him for a coward. Add to this the prudence of a man with experience of real life, who shrinks from an overwhelmingly unequal contest, preferring not to have to do with superior powers whether they be in number, in organization, or of the law. Hence his advice to his master, after the adventure of the galley-slaves, to keep away from the roads frequented by the Holy Brotherhood. This prudence before superior forces, carried further, turns into a real fear of supernatural powers or, simply, of the unknown. It has been a great mistake to make Sancho out a coward because he trembled before many dangers which to us seem puerile. Courage must be measured in relation to a subjective estimate of the enemy, and if in his ignorance, superstition, and simple-mindedness Sancho saw danger where we do not, our right to hold him a simpleton does not authorize us to brand him a coward. This observation should be enough to clear Sancho of the odium of dishonour for his attitude in certain adventures, like that of the fulling-mills, the apparition of Merlin, and others in which fear entered into him by way of the brain, the weak point of the ignorant. Proof that the origin of this weakness of Sancho was purely of the intellect and of the imagination is that he always in these cases takes refuge with the Duchess:

As for Sancho, it is enough to say, that fear carried him to his usual refuge, which was the duchess's side, or the skirts of her petticoat . . . (Part II, Chapter xxxvi.)

These traits of the personality of Sancho which have to do with his cowardice or valour come out with remarkable clearness in the adventure of the Knight of the Wood, Part II, Chapter xiv. When the unknown squire expresses his admiration of Sanchica Panza in coarse if naïve terms, Sancho feels the tide of anger rising in him:

'. . . and speak more civilly; for in a man brought up as you have been, among knights-errant . . ., I do not find those words becoming.'

Observe, then, his virile feelings awakened. Presently, when the sly squire proposes that, while their masters fight they also should set to, 'as is the custom in Andalucia', Sancho refuses point-blank to fight in cold blood, that is to fight like a fool. (Note in passing that such firm decisions are not typical of the coward.) And he says:

'. . . I shall not be so discourteous, nor so ungrateful, as to have any quarrel at all, be it never so little, with anyone, after having eaten of his bread, and drunk of his drink; besides, without anger, and without provocation, who the devil can set about dry fighting?'

But the Squire of the Wood, falling perhaps into the common error of mistaking Sancho's prudence for cowardice, makes bold to say:

'If that be all . . . I will provide a sufficient remedy; which is, that before we begin to combat, I will come up to your worship, and fairly give you three or four good cuffs, which will lay you flat at my feet, and awaken your choler, though it slept sounder than a dormouse.'

With these words the imprudent squire touches our man right on his chest, provoking an answer no less firm and decided for being moderate and calm:

'Against that trick I have another . . . not a whit behind it: I will take a good cudgel, and, before you reach me to awaken my choler, I will beat yours so sound asleep, that it shall never awake more but in another world, where it is well known I am not a man to let anybody handle my face; and let every one take heed to the arrow; though the safest way would be to let each man's choler sleep; no one knows what is in the soul of any one, and some go out for wool, who come home shorn; and God blessed peace, and cursed brawls; for if a cat, pursued, and pent in a room, and hard put to it, turns into a lion, God knows what I (that am a man) may turn into . . .'

But the workings of Sancho's mind do not stop short at this somewhat curious episode. Cervantes is still to show him to us under the influence of real fear, called forth by an unknown and, for him, supernatural danger. Dawn comes and the unfortunate man becomes aware of the gigantic nose of the Squire of the Wood:

In a word, it is said to have been an excessive size, hawked in the middle, and full of warts, of a strong purple colour like a mulberry; it hung two fingers' breadth below his mouth, and the size, colour, warts, and crookedness so disfigured his face, that Sancho, at sight thereof, began to tremble hand and foot, like a child in a fit, and resolved within himself to take two hundred cuffs before his choler should awaken to encounter that hobgoblin.

Here, then, compressed into one single episode, we get the whole field of Sancho's psychology concerning courage. Vigorous and virile by temperament, he becomes angry somewhat easily; prudent and cautious by common sense and experience, he avoids unequal and useless combats; childish and simple by nature and ignorance, he trembles before the unknown and the supernatural. Taking him all in all, a worthy brother of the knight he accompanies in life.

And this Don Quixote himself corroborates in the scene which follows. The Barber—of the helmet of Mambrino—enters the Inn and on seeing Don Quixote and, above all, Sancho who was 'mending something about the pack-saddle' of which he (Sancho) had despoiled him, he fell on Sancho saying:

'. . . Ah! mister thief, I have got you. Give me my basin and my pack-saddle, with all the furniture you robbed me of.'

Sancho, finding himself attacked so unexpectedly, and hearing the opprobrious language given him, with one hand held fast the pack-saddle, and with the other gave the barber such a dowse, that he bathed his mouth in blood. But for all that the barber did not let go his hold: on the contrary, he raised his voice in such a manner, that all the folks of the Inn ran together at the noise of the scuffle; and he cried out: 'Help, in the king's name, and in the name of justice; for this rogue and highway-robber would murder me for endeavouring to recover my own goods.'

'You lie,' answered Sancho, 'I am no highway-robber: my master Don Quixote won these spoils in fair war.'

Don Quixote was now present and not a little pleased to see how well his squire performed both on the defensive and offensive, *and from thenceforward took him for a man of mettle, and resolved in his mind to dub him a knight the first opportunity that offered, thinking the order of chivalry would be very well bestowed upon him.*

SANCHO'S FAITH

Let us try to see clearly what the character of Sancho is, now that we have eliminated from the picture the stain of cowardice which superficial observers thought they saw in him. Sancho's combativeness has after all the same limits as his personality, and those who have thought him a coward have done so because they did not realize that they were expecting to find Sancho's courage where Sancho himself could not be. The basis of his personality is that sound empirical common sense, that spontaneous wisdom which goes in England by the name of mother-wit. This natural gift is wont to be almost infallible when exercised on the concrete positive and tangible facts of everyday life. In this way is explained Sancho's success as a judge in the island of Barataria, when those who came to laugh stayed to admire. But once he gets away from the concrete, the man of sound common sense, for lack of the light of abstract reason, wanders like a blind man burdened rather than helped by his store of experience. Such is Sancho, perfectly described in a suggestive Spanish phrase: 'a sack of truths', i.e. truths without organic co-ordination, loose like stones in a sack. This is the inner significance of the strings of proverbs, in season and out, which Sancho threads into his speeches, as Don Quixote himself suggests when he calls him 'nothing but a sackful of proverbs and sly remarks'. (Part II, Chapter xliii.)

The contrast between his certainty and wisdom when faced with the concrete, and his incapacity and childishness when faced with the abstract, constitutes the basis of Sancho's character. Ideas incarnated in material bodies Sancho handles with assurance. But his mind becomes paralysed when it enters the kingdom of abstract thoughts, phantoms, and enchanters, beings which, in his confused head, he would probably put under the same category. The reader of *Don Quixote* will find a very apt illustration of this incapacity of Sancho to reason in the abstract in that diverting scene in which the Duchess makes the Squire confess that the enchantment of Dulcinea, which he himself had invented, is real and actual. For want of a general criterion, Sancho finds himself drawn by circumstances of the moment to conclusions of the moment. Hence a certain incoherence in him without which it is impossible to understand the real meaning of his faith in Don Quixote. Don Quixote's attitude to his own destiny is that of secret uncertainty held down and conquered by a continued effort of will, inspired in its turn by his imagination. The attitude of Sancho towards the transcendent person of his master is a continual coming and going from belief to unbelief. Sancho disbelieves every time he puts Don Quixote's theories to the proof of a concrete fact. Thus his protest in the case of Mambrino's helmet:

'As God liveth, Sir Knight of the Sorrowful Figure, I cannot endure nor bear with patience some things your worship says: they are enough to make me think, that all you tell me of chivalry, and of winning kingdoms and empires, of bestowing islands, and doing other favours and bounties according to the custom of knights-errant, must be mere wind and lies and all friction, or fiction, or how do you call it? for, to hear you say, that a barber's basin is Mambrino's helmet, and that you cannot be beaten out of this error in several days, what can one think, but that he, who says and affirms such a thing, must be crack-brained?'

There is a similar scene when Sancho finds out who really and truly is the person whom his master calls Dulcinea.

On the other hand, he comes back to his belief again when reasoned into it by ideas which sound well even though he does not understand them, as well as when confronted by a concrete fact which it is possible to explain by knight-errantry. Observe these movements of his mind, oscillating between credulity and incredulity, in the adventure of the wine-skins. He hears the Curate reproaching the Innkeeper for his belief in Books of Chivalry and, adds Cervantes:

> Sancho came in about the middle of this conversation, and was much confounded, and very pensive at what he heard said, that knights-errant were not now in fashion, and that all books of chivalry were mere lies and fooleries; and he resolved with himself to wait the event of this expedition of his master's; and if it did not succeed as happily as he expected, he would determine to leave him, and return home to his wife and children, and to his accustomed labour. (Part I, Chapter xxxii.)

A decision which does not prevent his coming out excitedly a little later from the garret shouting that his master had slashed the giant with his sword, cutting his head right off as if it were a turnip, because, as he says afterwards, he saw the blood running out of the body as from a fountain.

Observe how in all these cases Sancho's faith vacillates when he comes into direct contact with a person whom he regards as his superior. The Duchess, by merely stating it, makes him confess, if not even believe, that Dulcinea is enchanted. The Curate's arguments to the Innkeeper strike an indirect blow to his faith. Cervantes was careful to mark how concrete and empirical, how personal and direct was the beginning of both the faith and the incredulity of Sancho. The passage is worth quoting. Don Quixote has just been holding forth to the amateur shepherds and the professional goatherds on the virtues and utility of knight-errantry and on the beauty and lineage of Dulcinea. And Cervantes adds:

They all listened with great attention to the dialogue between these two: and even the goatherds and shepherds perceived the notorious distraction of our Don Quixote. Sancho Panza alone believed all that his master said to be true, knowing who he was, and having been acquainted with him from his birth. But what he somewhat doubted of was, what concerned the fair Dulcinea del Toboso: for no such a name or princess had ever come to his hearing, though he lived so near Toboso. (Part I, Chapter xiii.)

In short, Sancho is sunk in perplexity. He feels himself bound to Don Quixote by a deep and sincere affection which Cervantes makes him express with touching frankness and simplicity:

'Mine is not so,' answered Sancho: 'I can assure you, he has nothing of the knave in him; on the contrary, he is a simple soul; knows not how to do ill to any, but good to all; bears no malice; a child may persuade him it is night at noonday: and for this simplicity I love him as my life, and cannot find in my heart to leave him, let him commit never so many extravagances.' (Part II, Chapter xiii.)

But there is in addition cemented into his affection, as it were, another more material element which Sancho reveals to us with his habitual sincerity, habitual even in his slyness and deceit. His master has promised him an island and, even in the indisputable realm of tangible reality, he himself once came upon a purse of a hundred gold ducats in the Sierra Morena. Rarely has the fascination of wealth been more vividly expressed than in Sancho's confession to the Squire of the Wood:

'. . . I beseech God to deliver me from mortal sin, for it will be no less if he takes me away from this dangerous profession of a squire into which I have run a second time, enticed and deluded by a purse of a hundred ducats, which I found one day in the midst of the Sierra Morena; and the devil is continually setting before my eyes, here and there, and everywhere, a bag full of gold pistoles, so that methinks, at every step, I am laying my hand upon it, embracing it, and carrying it home, buying lands, settling rents, and living like a prince: and all the while this runs in my head, all the toils I undergo with this crazy master of mine, who to my knowledge is more of the madman than of the knight, become supportable and easy to me.' (Part II, Chapter xiii.)

This passage leaves no doubt as to the material nature of Sancho's ambition, and there are many others to confirm it. But it is sufficient also to establish that there is no more materialism in him than what is indispensable to a mind working step by step on the slow road of experience; for the desire for wealth of the man who dreams of buying lands, settling rents, and living like a prince is not without loftiness. Not for nothing does he incarnate his ambition in the governing of an island. What at bottom he wants is not wealth but power.

Power is to Sancho what glory is to his master. Just as Dulcinea personifies glory to Don Quixote, the island materializes power to Sancho. And just as Don Quixote has to believe in Dulcinea in order to believe in himself,

Sancho has to believe in Don Quixote in order to believe in the island. Thus the faith of the knight, after supporting his own spirit, feeds the spirit of the servant.

Once this delusion has nested in his head, Sancho is true brother to Don Quixote, more fortunate only in that when in doubt he has but to draw on his master's faith, while the Knight of the Sorrowful Figure must draw his out of the well of his own spirit by sheer strength of will.

Sancho must believe or his island will vanish. Such is the pathetic meaning of that melancholy remark of his when the Innkeeper points out to him that the giant whom Don Quixote thinks he has slain is but a wine-skin.

'I know nothing; only that I should be so unfortunate, that, for want of finding this head, my earldom will melt away like salt in water.' (Part I, Chapter xxxv.)

He must believe, and like Don Quixote he goes about unconsciously looking here, there, and everywhere for reasons to strengthen his belief. His standby is his personal faith in Don Quixote as a superior being in knowledge, courage, rank, and example. Sancho repeatedly expresses his admiration for his master's gifts: his powers of speech, his store of knowledge, his style, in short all that we should nowadays put together under the label of 'culture'. He often puts this forward as an argument that his master is not mad; an argument addressed to others but in reality aimed at himself. For the main thing is to save the island.

In spite of everything, Sancho wins his island, loses it disillusioned, and still continues by the side of Don

Quixote. From which we see that there has been growing between these two something deeper, something which was of course already there, latent in these two heroes at birth : the fraternity of soul which unites this strange master and this singular servant. A brother in illusion to Don Quixote, Sancho has to follow him along the road to perfection until death—the death of illusion which is sanity.

Don Quixote's Influence on Sancho

FREED from the rigidity which has simplified them into two antithetical and symmetrical characters, Don Quixote and Sancho, to the eye of the attentive observer, take on the lifelike and human mobility which they inherit from their most human father and creator. The same sap flows through their actions, the same spirit interpenetrates them, and so they draw gradually nearer, attracting each other by virtue of a slow and sure mutual influence which is, in its inspiration and its development, the great charm and achievement of the book.

The first to show this influence is Sancho. You remember that delightful scene with his wife, Teresa, when he tries to break to her the news that he has decided to sally forth again with the Knight-errant:

The translator of this history, coming to write his fifth chapter (Part II), says he takes it to be apocryphal, because in it Sancho talks in another style than could be expected from his shallow understanding, and says such subtle things, that he reckons impossible that he should know them . . .

So speaks **Cervantes**, pointing out the fact but, after his masterly fashion, not revealing the subtle reason for such high falutin phrases on the lips, and such far-fetched reasons in the mind, of his squire. Revelations like these, which the utilitarian modern author states plainly, are always in Cervantes woven into the fabric itself or, at most, indicated in a phrase of the dialogue as in Teresa Panza's exclamation:

'Look you, Sancho, ever since you have been a member of a knight-errant, you talk in such a roundabout manner, that there is nobody understands you.'

These words are the key to the scene. Sancho echoing Don Quixote, imitates with rustic simplicity—and simplicity working hard ends in complication—the arabesques of style and thought of his master, the reasons of his unreason :

'Dear wife, if it were God's will, I should be very glad not to be so well pleased as I appear to be.'

But his imitation of his master does not stop short at thought and diction. His whole attitude to his wife in this scene is a replica of that of Don Quixote towards himself; superior, patronizing, instructive, now conciliating and patient, now angry and domineering, and always condescending. The very words which Sancho utters indignantly to his obstinate wife are a faithful echo of Don Quixote's outbursts against his obdurate squire :

'Certainly you must have some familiar in that body of yours; heavens bless thee, woman! what a parcel of things have you been stringing one upon another, without either proverbs to do with what I am saying? Hark you, fool, and head or tail! What have Cascajo, the brooches, or the ignorant . . .'

That nothing may be missing he goes even to the point of correcting her language. Says Teresa, resigned to her fate :

'And if you are revolved to do as you say . . .'
'Resolved, you should say, wife, and not revolved.'

And all—the delicious irony of it!—all to convert Teresa to a belief in islands and earldoms, just as Don

Quixote's efforts are directed to make him believe in windmills and castles. This scene, in which the parallel between the two finds such delightful expression, is one of the jewels of the book, one of those passages full of subtle echoes and harmonies that only great creators can achieve.

Thus we see Sancho modelling himself externally on Don Quixote. But the inner imitation is no less profound. There is nothing more instructive than the gradual shipwreck of our shrewd peasant's common sense in the sea of fantasy over which his master makes him venture. We know, now, that Sancho, like his master, is dominated by a concrete delusion symbolical of an abstract delusion. For Sancho the island materializes power, just as for Don Quixote Dulcinea personifies glory. Hence their fraternity, the parallelism between them. But the lines of their respective destinies, which start as parallels, are attracted to one another by mutual sympathy. The star of Don Quixote influences that of Sancho and, by virtue of the law of attraction, we see the one whose ambition is for concrete things little by little feeling the lure of less material satisfactions. Vanity, the lighter side of glory, steals unexpectedly into his soul when he least thinks it and rapidly becomes mistress of it.

Note, in passing, the marvellous skill with which Cervantes uses the success of his first Part to enrich his characters in the second. When we meet the Knight and the Squire in Part II, they are already famous. The scene in which bachelor Sanson Carrasco comments with them on the published history of Don Quixote marks a capital moment in the life of Sancho. The field of his life suddenly widens as he feels a pleasure till then new to him. For the first time he tastes of that sweet wine of fame, the mere aroma of which was enough to take his master afield. And be it remarked, in passing, how consistently Cervantes shows us empirical Sancho totally ignorant of what glory is until it actually breaks upon him by direct experience; while imaginative Don Quixote creates it out of nothing, pure and spotless from his own immaculate mind. All of which explains their respective attitudes before the actual glory which the Bachelor reveals to them. Don Quixote, mistrustful, fearing instinctively that actual glory will not be so pure and beautiful as imagined glory; Sancho, on the other hand, yielding himself ingenuously to the satisfaction of this new pleasure.

The movements of Sancho's mind in this chapter are observed and delineated by a master hand. Vanity pricks him from the first moment. Already in the previous chapter, when he announces to his master that there is a printed history of his adventures going about, called *The Ingenious Gentleman Don Quixote de la Mancha*, he gives the first sign of his new foible, adding immediately :

'. . . and he says, it mentions me too by my very name of Sancho Panza . . .'

Hardly has he informed his master of this, than he offers spontaneously to go 'on wings' to fetch Sanson Carrasco to get more details from him about the book. Nevertheless, Sancho is able to contain and even, at the beginning, to hide the interest now awakened in his soul, under a layer of indifference as of a barely curious spectator. His first interventions in the conversation between his master and the Bachelor are merely to point out inaccuracies, or ask questions prompted by a bashful interest. Sancho draws attention to the fact that the author speaks of 'Doña Dulcinea'; or asks if there is any reference in the book to the adventure of the Yangüeses. But when Sanson Carrasco alludes to Sancho's 'capers in the blanket', the Squire comes forward and it is not long before he claims the first role. Interrupting the abstract discussion between Sanson and Don Quixote as to whether or not an historian ought to relate everything that happens, Sancho gives a tug to the conversation in the direction of his own concrete interests:

'Well, if it be so that that Señor Moor is in a vein of truth telling, there is no doubt but among my master's rib-roastings, mine are to be found also . . .'

From this he leaps several steps at once and declares himself one of the main characters in the story:

'. . . for I hear that I am one of the principal *parsons* in it.'

The crescendo is kept up vigorously to the end of the scene:

'Another corrector of hard words! . . .'
'Before God, sir, if I am not fit to govern an island at these years, I shall not know how to govern it at the age of Methusalem. The mischief of it is, that the said island sticks I know not where, and not in my want of a head-piece to govern it.'
'I have seen governors ere now, who, in my opinion, do not come up to the sole of my shoe; and yet they are called your lordship, and are served on plate.'

So the good Sancho goes on blowing himself out with fame and importance until he ends by including himself and his master in a common plural, with himself first, and declaring that he is ready to give the learned Moor material for a second Part and to spur his master on to make another sally. This outburst, typical of the intoxication of glory which now possesses the once phlegmatic squire, opens, characteristically, with a condemnation of things done for material gain :

'Does the author aim at money and profit? It will be a wonder then if he succeeds, since he will only stitch it away in great haste like a tailor on Easter-eve; for works that are done hastily are never finished with that perfection they require. I wish this same Señor Moor would consider a little what he is about : for I and my master will furnish him so abundantly with lime and mortar in matter of adventures and variety of accidents, that he may not only compile a second part, but a hundred. The good man thinks, without doubt, that we lie sleeping here in straw; but let him hold up the foot while the smith is shoeing, and he will see on which we halt. What I can say is that if this master of mine had taken my counsel, we had ere now been in the field, redressing grievances, and righting wrongs, as is the practice and usage of good knights-errant.'

Here we are in the presence of a more ambitious Sancho, a Sancho who feels himself in a way on a level with his master. Though at the end of Chapter vii, he falls into tears and sighs when Don Quixote accepts the services of Sanson Carrasco as squire, this fall is in itself a fall due to pride, for the Sancho who provokes the conflict by asking his master for a fixed salary is not the humble apprentice squire of yore, but a master squire who knows that his name is famous.

As an illustration of the precision with which this novel was thought out, it may be worth pointing out that it was precisely after this scene that Sancho puzzled his wife Teresa by suddenly addressing her in the high falutin and incomprehensible style commented on at the beginning of this chapter.

In the rest of the second part Cervantes does not cease to point out, either directly or indirectly, the vanity which has wrought such havoc in Sancho's heart, and has lightened his positive soul with something of the chimerical spirit which moves his master: thus in Chapter viii, talking to Don Quixote, the squire says:

'That is what I say too; and I take it for granted, in that same legend or history of us, the bachelor Carrasco tells us he has seen, my reputation is tossed about like a tennis-ball, here and there and as one might say, sweeping the streets. Now, as I am an honest man, I never spoke ill of any enchanter, nor have I wealth enough to be envied. It is true, indeed, I am said to be somewhat sly, and to have a little spice of the knave; but the grand cloak of my simplicity, always natural and never artificial, hides and covers all. And if I had nothing else to boast of, but the believing, as I do always, firmly and truly in God, and in all that the holy Catholic Roman Church holds and believes, and the being, as I really am, a mortal enemy to the Jews, historians ought to have mercy upon me, and treat me well in their writings. But let them say what they will; naked was I born, and naked I am: I neither lose nor win; and, so my name be but in print, and go about the world from hand to hand, I care not a fig, let people say of me whatever they list.'

Bear in mind also in this connexion Sancho's attitude on meeting the Knight of the Wood, Chapter xii. Sancho thrusts himself into the conversation between the two knights, whereupon the Knight of the Wood says:

'I never in my life saw a squire who durst presume to talk, where his lord was talking . . .

'In faith I have talked, and can talk, before one as good as —, and perhaps —, but let that rest; for the more you stir it —.'

And not content with this protest he at once seeks satisfaction for his offended pride, saying to the Squire of the Wood, who had proposed that they should move off to a distance to talk after the manner of squires:

'With all my heart, and I will tell you who I am, that you may see whether I am fit to enter in a dozen with the most eminent squires *parlant*.'

More characteristic, if possible, of this interpenetration of Sancho and Don Quixote in their common craving for glory and at the same time of the growing ambition of our good squire, is that interrogatory through which the servant puts his master as to the relative value of the glory to be achieved by holiness or by knight-errantry, in the course of which, taking, be it noted, the intellectual initiative, he reaches the following conclusion in which the collective plural *we* should be remarked:

'I mean that *we* had better turn saints, and we shall then the sooner attain to *that renown we aim at*.' (Chapter viii.)

These words already betray such a rise in Sancho's spirit that Cervantes' observation at the beginning of Chapter viii does not surprise us:

Don Quixote and Sancho remained by themselves; and scarcely was Sanson parted from them, when Rocinante began to neigh, and Rucio to sigh; which was held by both knight and squire for a good sign, and a most happy omen, though if the truth were to be told, the sighs and brayings of the ass exceeded the neighings of the steed; from whence Sancho gathered that his good luck was to surpass and get above that of his master.

And so in truth it was to be. For, while Sancho's spirit rises from reality to illusion, Don Quixote's descends from illusion to reality. And the two curves cross in that saddest of adventures, one of the cruellest in the book, when Sancho enchants Dulcinea, bringing the most noble of knights, for love of the purest illusion, to his knees before the most repulsive of realities: a Dulcinea coarse, uncouth, and reeking of garlic.

Sancho's Influence on Don Quixote

WHILE Sancho, smitten with love of fame, 'that last infirmity of noble minds', gradually rises towards the Knight-errant, life's hard treatment gradually wears the Knight down to the squire. It is a slow and subtle evolution which Cervantes prepares and develops with consummate skill.

Perhaps the first symptoms of it may be found in the tendency, new in Don Quixote, to consider ways and means. Part II shows us a Don Quixote travelling with money and provisions:

> In short, in those three days, Don Quixote and Sancho furnished themselves with what they thought convenient, and . . . took the road to Toboso; Don Quixote upon his good Rocinante, and Sancho upon his old Rucio, his wallets stored with provisions, and his purse with money, which Don Quixote had given him against whatever might happen.

In this second part of the book, Don Quixote no longer relies on his privileges as knight-errant, but pays his fare at the inns like any ordinary mortal. The Don Quixote of Part II is no longer sallying forth spontaneously but pushed thereto by Don Quixote of Part I, a clear case, if you will, of the saying *noblesse oblige*. Cervantes lays stress on this point when describing the manner in which the Knight reaches his decision to sally forth a third time. He is stimulated first by the conversation with Sanson Carrasco which so greatly raises the spirits of the squire and of the Knight. Secondly, Sancho launches his enthusiastic appeal which in itself is a call to arms:

'. . . that if this master of mine had taken my counsel, we had ere now been in the field, redressing grievances, and righting wrongs, as is the practice and usage of good knights-errant.'

And lastly even Rocinante comes on the scene to infuse courage into his master.

Sancho had scarcely finished this discourse, when the neighings of Rocinante reached their ears; which Don Quixote took for a most happy omen, and resolved to make another sally within three or four days; and declaring his intention to the bachelor, he asked his advice which way he should begin his journey.

Everything then combines to impel to renewed adventuring this Don Quixote of Part II, a little passive and reluctant, so different from that bold and resolute paladin of the two first sallies. Notice how he asks the Bachelor's advice as to when he should begin his journey, and how, before carrying out his resolve, there is still another fervent harangue by the Bachelor:

'Go on then, dear Señor Don Quixote, beautiful and brave; and let your worship and grandeur lose no time, but set forward rather to-day than to-morrow . . .'

Call to mind the last chapters of Part I in which Don Quixote has already had to draw on his faith as the prodigal lives on his capital:

For, if on the one side, you tell me that the priest and the barber of our village bear us company, and, on the other side, I find myself locked up in a cage, and know of myself that no force but that which is supernatural could be sufficient to imprison me . . .'

This ending of the first Part already forebodes the approaching spiritual impoverishment of the hero, as seen in the passivity of his mind at the beginning of the second Part. A consummate master of psychology, Cervantes depicts in his depressed Don Quixote that mood of quiet and serene humour which usually steals over the soul like a moon which follows and takes the place of the sun of faith. There is already a hint of it in that answer which he gave to his niece when she expressed her admiration for his eloquence:

'I assure you, niece, that if these knightly thoughts did not employ all my senses, there is nothing I could not do, nor any curious art but what I could turn my hand to, especially bird-cages and tooth-picks.'

But the most subtle and profound illustration of this frame of mind is that where Don Quixote, with a silent smile, falls in with the conditions his petulant squire imposes on him in the matter of style. Sancho says to his master:

'Sir, I have now reluced my wife to consent to let me go with your worship wherever you please to carry me.'

'Reduced, you should say, Sancho,' quoth Don Quixote, 'and not reluced.'

'Once or twice already,' answered Sancho, 'if I remember right, I have besought your worship not to mend my words, if you understand my meaning; and when you do not, say: "Sancho, or devil, I understand you not," and if I do not explain myself, then you may correct me; for I am so focile . . .'

'I do not understand you, Sancho,' said Don Quixote, 'for I know not the meaning of focile.'

'So focile,' answered Sancho, 'means, I am so much so.'

'I understand you less now,' replied Don Quixote.

'Why, if you do not understand me,' answered Sancho, 'I know not how to express it; I know no more, God help me.'

'O! now I have it,' answered Don Quixote: 'you mean you are so docile, so pliant, and so tractable, that you will readily comprehend whatever I shall say to you, and will learn whatever I shall teach you.'

'I will lay a wager,' quoth Sancho, 'that you took me from the beginning, and understood me perfectly; only you had a mind to put me out, to hear me make two hundred blunders more.'

'That may be,' replied Don Quixote : 'but, in short, what says Teresa?'

'Teresa,' quoth Sancho, 'says, that fast bind fast find, and that we must have less talking and more doing; for he who shuffles is not he who cuts, and one performance is worth two promises : and, say I, there is but little in woman's advice, yet he that won't take it is not over-wise.'

'I say so too,' replied Don Quixote : 'proceed, Sancho, for you talk admirably to-day.'

'The case is,' replied Sancho, 'that, as your worship very well knows, we are all mortal, here to-day, and gone to-morrow; that the lamb goes to the spit as soon as the sheep; and that nobody can promise himself in this world more hours of life than God pleases to give him : for death is deaf, and, when he knocks at life's door, is always in haste; and nothing can stay him, neither force, nor entreaties, nor sceptres, nor mitres, according to public voices and report, and according to what is told us from our pulpits.'

'All this is true,' said Don Quixote : 'but I do not perceive what you would be at.'

'What I would be at,' quoth Sancho, 'is, that your worship would be pleased to appoint me a certain salary, at so much per month, for the time I shall serve you, and the said salary be paid me out of your estate; for I have no mind to stand to the courtesy of recompenses, which come late, or lame, or never, God help me with my own. In short, I would know what I am to get, be it little or much : for the hen sits if it be but upon one egg, and many little ones make a mickle, and while one is getting something, one is losing nothing. In good truth, should it fall out (which I neither believe nor despair of) that your

worship should give me that same island you have promised me, I am not so ungrateful, nor am I for making so
hard a bargain, as not to consent, that the amount of the
rent of such island be appraised, and my salary be deducted
at a fair rake.'

'Friend Sancho,' answered Don Quixote, 'there are times
when a rate is as good as a rake.'

'I understand you,' quoth Sancho; 'I will lay a wager, I
should have said rate, and not rake: but that signifies
nothing, since your worship knew my meaning.' (Part II,
Chapter vii.)

It would be difficult to express more happily that
mood of quiet humour which accompanies disillusionment in noble minds. Cervantes with his marvellous
sense of opportunity presents it as the fruition of the
physical and moral repose which follows the second
sally. The hardships of the third are to disturb not a
little the purity and serenity of this humour, which
misfortune will turn to bitterness. For, in this third
sally, there occurs the adventure of the enchantment
of Dulcinea, through which the spirit of Don Quixote,
vanquished by that of Sancho, enters finally on its
decline.

Sancho, finding himself in a tight corner when
Don Quixote brings him to El Toboso in search of
Dulcinea, coolly decides to deceive his master in that
inimitable soliloquy under a tree while his master is
waiting for him in the wood. The method which his
fancy hits on is simple but excellent and consists in
asserting, swearing, and reasserting. Sancho has learnt
it from his master, who, by similar methods, tried so
often to impose his own chimeras upon him. When the
wily squire, by sheer power of will, forces an uncouth
peasant girl on his master as Dulcinea, Don Quixote,

on bended knees beside Sancho, 'with staring and disturbed eyes, looked wistfully at her, whom Sancho called queen, and lady . . .' For it was the lot of the Knight to undergo a destiny the opposite of that he strove to impress on others. While the vision which he held as reality was more beautiful than the real, the reality which Sancho presented to him as vision was an insult to his dreams.

The delicate interplay of moods between master and man, following this adventure, is sketched by a master hand. Don Quixote suffers at first from a profound depression, which Sancho tries to combat by words of comfort which savour of incipient remorse:

'It may be so,' answered Sancho; 'for her beauty confounded me, as much as her deformity did your worship. But let us trust all to God, who alone knows what shall befall in this vale of tears, this evil world we have here, in which there is scarce anything to be found without some mixture of iniquity, imposture, or knavery.'

Withal, Sancho's personality, which has already grown more vigorous, comes out of the adventure reinforced. It is not he, now, who draws sustenance from his master's spirit, but Don Quixote who leans on the spirit of his squire: thus in the same page we find again that collective plural wherewith Sancho puts himself on a level with his master:

'. . . we, for our part, will make a shift, and bear it as well as we can, pursuing our adventures . . .'

The next adventure, that of the Chariot of the Parliament of Death, shows us Don Quixote somewhat slack and discouraged, ready to hear and accept explanations, having lost that imagination of his which in other days could transform every event into an adventure, his spirit already prepared for disillusionment:

'Upon the faith of a knight-errant,' answered Don Quixote, 'when I first espied this cart, I imagined some grand adventure offered itself; and I say now, that it is necessary to lay one's hand upon appearances to be undeceived. God be with you, good people: go, and act your play, and if there be anything in which I may be of service to you, command me; for I will do it readily, and with a good will, for, ever since I was a boy, I loved the "Mask" and my eyes longed after the players.'

And, if it be true that the treatment meted out to Rucio at the hands of a fool in the troop roused his old energy in the Knight, it is no less true that he lets himself be guided by Sancho's advice and agrees to retreat when matters begin to look ugly.

In the next chapter Sancho has an attack of eloquence which shows the rise in his self-esteem and satisfaction, as well as the growing influence of Don Quixote, as he himself declares in his delightful jargon:

'And good reason why,' answered Sancho; 'for some of your worship's discretion must needs stick to me, as lands, that in themselves are barren and dry, by dunging and cultivating come to bear good fruit. My meaning is, that your worship's conversation has been the dung laid upon the barren soil of my dry understanding, and the cultivation has been the time I have been in your service, and in your company; and by that I hope to produce fruit like any blessing, and such as will not disparage or deviate from the seeds of good breeding, which your worship has sown in my shallow understanding.'

At this point there occurs the adventure of the Knight of the Mirrors, which gives some variety to the hitherto simple movement of Sancho's rise, and Don Quixote's fall. Sancho, terrified by the supernatural nose of the Squire of the Wood, feels himself caught between fear and simplicity, with its accompanying humiliation. As for Don Quixote, he continues to show the same quiet humour born of disillusionment which we have seen in him since the beginning of Part II. The mention of Dulcinea's name, or his own, no longer rouses him to excitement, as even lesser things were wont to do in the past. He bides his time patiently, and when he does protest he is moderate though firm. But when fate gives him the victory the tide of his spirit rises once more momentarily in his soul and, with his faith of old, he makes himself, and even Sancho, believe in the enchantment of the vanquished foe in order to explain how the face of the bachelor Carrasco could appear under the vizor of the Knight of the Wood. This success renders Don Quixote 'content, proud, and vainglorious', by which Cervantes suggests that this rise in Don Quixote's spirits is not very deep but partakes rather of the nature of excitement. Thus we see him loquacious and communicative towards the Knight of the Green Riding-coat; vain, when he exclaims 'Your lion-whelps to me!' in the adventure of the lions, and ironical and barely polite when he rejects on this adventure the counsels of prudence of the Knight of the Green Riding-coat. This is the mood expressed in his words to Sancho after the happy ending of the adventure of the lions:

'What think you of this, Sancho?' quoth Don Quixote: 'can any enchantments prevail against true courage? With ease may the enchanters deprive me of good fortune; but of courage and resolution they never can.'

But, as the effects of the victory over the Knight of the Wood wear off, the minds of both master and servant return to their normal rhythm. So we see Sancho impatiently answering back when his master corrects his speech:

'Criticizing, I suppose, you would say,' quoth Don Quixote, 'and not cricketizing, thou misapplier of good language, whom God confound.'
'Pray, sir, be not so sharp upon me,' answered Sancho; 'for you know I was not bred at court, nor have studied in Salamanca, to know whether I add to, or take a letter from my words. As God shall save me, it is unreasonable to expect, that the Sayaguese should speak like the Toledans; nay, there are Toledans, who are not over nice in the business of speaking politely.' (Chapter xix.)

preaching to him eloquently:

'In good faith, sir,' answered Sancho, 'there is no trusting to Madam Skeleton, I mean Death, who devours lambs as well as sheep: and I have heard our vicar say she treads with equal foot on the lofty towers of kings and the humble cottages of the poor. That same gentlewoman is more powerful than nice: she is not at all squeamish: she eats of everything and lays hold of all; and stuffs her wallets with people of all sorts, of all ages, and pre-eminences. She is not a reaper that sleeps away the noon-day heat; for she cuts down and mows, at all hours, the dry as well as the green grass: nor does she stand to chew, but devours and swallows down all that comes in her way; for she has a canine appetite that is never satisfied; and, though she has no belly, she makes it appear that she has a perpetual dropsy; and a thirst to drink down the lives of

all that live, as one would drink a jug of cold water.'
(Chapter xx.)

and even offended when Don Quixote alludes to his
alleged pusillanimity :

'Good your worship, judge of your own chivalries,'
answered Sancho, 'and meddle not with judging of other
men's fears or valours; for perhaps I am as pretty a
fearer of God as any of my neighbours : and pray let
me whip off this scum; for all besides is idle talk, of
which we must give an account in the next world.' (*End
of* Chapter xx.)

Don Quixote, on his side, reveals the uneasiness of
his mind in the discourse which he addresses to his
sleeping squire at the beginning of Chapter xx :

'O happy thou above all that live on the face of the
earth, who neither envying, nor being envied, sleepest on
with tranquillity of spirit ! neither do enchanters persecute, nor enchantments affright thee. Sleep on, I say
again, and will say a hundred times more, sleep on : for no
jealousies on thy lady's account keep thee in perpetual
watchings, nor do anxious thoughts of paying debts awake
thee, nor is thy rest broken with the thoughts of what thou
must do to-morrow, to provide for thyself and thy little
family. Ambition disquiets thee not, nor does the vain
pomp of the world disturb thee : for thy desires extend
not beyond the limits of taking care of thy ass : for that
of thy person is laid upon my shoulders, a counter-balance
and burden that nature and custom have laid upon
masters. The servant sleeps, and the master is waking, to
consider how he is to maintain, prefer, and do him kind-
nesses. The pain of seeing the obdurate heaven made, as it
were, of brass, and refusing convenient dews to refresh
the earth, afflicts not the servant, but the master, who is
bound to provide, in times of sterility and famine, for him
who served him in times of fertility and abundance.'

F

and the decline of his faith in the calm with which he hears and allows it to be said at Camacho's wedding that Quiteria is the most beautiful lady in the world :

> Which Don Quixote hearing, said to himself : 'It is plain these people have not seen my Dulcinea del Toboso; for, had they seen her, they would have been a little more upon the reserve in praising this Quiteria of theirs.'

The episode which symbolizes this decline is the curious adventure of the Cave of Montesinos.

The Cave of Montesinos

THE adventure of the Cave of Montesinos comes in as a sort of 'harmonic' of the whole book, an illusion within an illusion, like the seed within the fruit. In it Don Quixote touches the fringe of reality and appears to us partly in the sunshine of sound sense, partly in the shadow of madness. In the rest of the book we have seen him building up his faith as best he could, but keeping a discreet silence as to the origin of the materials which he brought to his task. Whatever their origin, they are made sound and true by the faith and will of the Knight. We observe, are silent, and acquiesce. But in the adventure of the Cave of Montesinos the veil which covers the intimate workings of Don Quixote is thinner. With how light and deft a hand Cervantes measures the exact degree of his revelations and the proportions of light and shade in his pictures! Though clearer than in other adventures, how delicately obscure he remains when dwelling on the strange adventure of the Cave of Montesinos! Like all the rest, this adventure shows us Don Quixote's soul as a field on which imagination, creator of chimeras, is battling with sense which devours them. But, whereas in the other adventures we beheld Don Quixote's will defending a chimera already created— or created on the instant in a magnificent 'it seems so and so it is'—here, in the Cave of Montesinos, we are witnessing the creative activity and the will working in unavowed co-operation. Is Don Quixote then lying? Not expressly and deliberately. But imaginative beings do not see the frontier between truth and falsehood so clearly as do those who have no more use for their imagination than have barnyard fowls for their wings. Shelley could not distinguish the real from the imaginary. Why should Don Quixote, whose imagination was no less intense than that of Shelley?

But this observation is not enough to account for the complexity of the Knight's attitude when he came out of the cave. If illusion and reality in this adventure are less well blended than in the others, it is because Don Quixote's faith is less intense. Consequently the collaboration of his will in transforming things is more conscious. The fact that he is aware of what he is doing, that he is doing it deliberately, is what makes this adventure unique in the life of our Knight. Cervantes leaves it to the judicious reader to decide whether it is apocryphal or true, 'though it is held for certain, that, upon his death-bed, he (Don Quixote) retracted'. There is much in Don Quixote's words and deeds, both before and after the adventure, to suggest that public rumour was not entirely off the track. To begin with, at the opening of the chapter (xxii) Cervantes puts a strange declaration of principle into the mouth of Don Quixote which it behoves us to emphasize. Remarking on Basilio's stratagem the Knight-errant says: 'It cannot nor ought to be called deceit, which aims at virtuous ends.'

Here we have the idea which is turning in the subterranean deeps of Don Quixote's mind when he sets out to explore the cave. Is it to be wondered at, then, that the Knight, thinking after this manner, is tempted in the solitude and silence of the fearful cave to plot a deceit with the virtuous object of regilding the scutcheon of his tarnished knight-errantry? His every word and act in this chapter help to bear out the state of depression in which, except for a few intervals, we have seen him since the beginning of Part II. Shortly after announcing the principle that the end justifies the means, Don Quixote himself counsels Basilio to 'quit the exercise of those abilities, wherein he so much excelled; for though they procured him fame, they got him no money': a notorious contrast with Sancho's apostrophe, quoted above, in which he censures the author of *Don Quixote* for working for money. But if the prelude to the adventure allows us to see the not very heroic state of mind in which Don Quixote sets out, the story which the Knight gives of it is more than proof that the Don Quixote of the Cave of Montesinos is a sad Don Quixote, beaten by reality, taught by experience, and strongly influenced by his squire.

The fact is that this story is the offspring of a secret and half-avowed compromise with reality. Our hero ceases to be altogether heroic, mingling a certain alloy of base utilitarian copper with the gold of his heroism. Hence that state of mind which this most strange story reveals. Pure-hearted beings, once they allow themselves to become tainted with impurity, evade the admission of it by taking refuge in humour, i.e. a state of mind in which they both are and are not, will and will not, at the same time. They lie and do not lie. Don Quixote tells his adventure seriously, but in a mood which seems to say: 'All this is in fun: if you believe it literally the fault is in your simplicity, not in my intention.'

This is the explanation why Don Quixote for the first and last time speaks facetiously of matters referring to knight-errantry. The whole story is adorned with exaggerations, ironical remarks and jests which, on Don Quixote's lips, would seem out of place were it not for the psychological circumstances mentioned. When describing Montesinos Don Quixote paints for us his 'rosary of beads . . . bigger than middling walnuts, and every tenth bead like an ordinary ostrich egg'. Then comes the episode of Durandarte's heart, so comic, so pointedly told by Don Quixote, the whole based on a ballad which Durandarte although dead declaims over his own tomb:

'O my dear cousin Montesinos! the last thing I desired of you, when I was dying, and my soul departing, was to carry my heart, ripping it out of my breast with a dagger, or poniard, to Belerma.'

In Montesinos' reply our Knight carries his humour to a strange length:

Long since, O my dearest cousin Durandarte, I did what you enjoined me in that bitter day of our loss: I took out your heart as well as I could, without leaving the least bit of it in your breast; I wiped it with a lace handkerchief, took it, and went off full speed with it for France, having first laid you in the bosom of the earth, shedding as many tears as sufficed to wash my hands, and clean away the blood stuck to them by raking in your entrails. By the same token, dear cousin of my soul, in the first place I lighted upon, going from Roncesvalles, I sprinkled a little salt over your heart, that it might not stink, and might keep, if not fresh, at least dried up, till it came to the lady Belerma.

Here we are taken straight into realism, and so merry a realism that we see at once the ravages which resignation has wrought in the heart of Don Quixote. In this atmosphere the unexpected reply of Durandarte:

'And though it should fall out otherwise,' answered the poor Durandarte with a faint and low voice, 'though it should not prove so, O cousin, I say patience, and shuffle the cards.'

causes no feeling of strangeness but only a comic surprise.

Don Quixote has still farther to go along this road leading away from his old idealism and delicacy. His description of Belerma takes him a step nearer the cruel realism of the epoch (and of all Spanish epochs) and even, in some of its details, borders on cynicism. The circumstances are such that they determine a coincidence between the momentary mood of the character and the normal or dominant bent of the author. Cervantes is a twofold nature; he is an idealist disillusioned, taking refuge in a human and indulgent humour; on the other hand, he is a clear-sighted realist with a touch of cynicism. His dominant mood is precisely the one to which the logic of his creative spirit was to bring Don Quixote in the course of this adventure. In such cases by natural law a psychological resonance is produced between the two, and the author inevitably influences his hero. The realism which Don Quixote unexpectedly reveals in this story is Cervantes' own, so rich and complex, at the same time human and cruel, reverent and cynical. So that in this adventure of the Cave of Montesinos Don Quixote comes nearer than ever to resembling that Don Miguel, knight-errant too after his fashion, to whom he owed his life.

The influence of Cervantes is clear in the scene which takes place in the cave between Don Quixote and Dulcinea. This is the second time that the Knight sees his lady enchanted, though in real life he had never

seen her. The first was on the road to Toboso, at the
moment when Sancho enchanted her by virtue of his
own wit and will. Nothing could be more instructive
than the contrast between Don Quixote's attitude on
these two occasions. On the road to Toboso Don
Quixote is tragic. On his knees before the shrew 'with
staring and disturbed eyes', the poor Knight addresses
to his illusion that pathetic appeal which comes to his
lips still fresh and perfumed by his most pure love. But
in the Cave of Montesinos his language is very different.
A characteristic fact : Don Quixote's imagination leads
him to fancy that Dulcinea, enchanted, is in need of
money and is sending him one of her companions to
raise some by pawning a dimity petticoat. This bringing into contact of Dulcinea, the symbol of illusion,
and money, the symbol of material force, is in itself a
piece of cruel realism. On the lips of Don Quixote it is
desolating and reveals the depth of the influence which
Sancho has already had on him. But Cervantes drives
his scepticism even further, for not only does he put
into the mind and words of the Knight of the Ideal
this merciless contrast of values; he presents him con-
templating it with relative calm, in fact almost coldly.
The message which Don Quixote sends to his lady is
measured and unmoved and, what is worse, presents
touches of a flippant humour which, from Don Quixote
to Dulcinea, would seem impossible.

Don Quixote a humorist; Don Quixote a realist; Don
Quixote irreverent ! Such are the surprising, if natural,
results of a moment of utilitarian weakness in the man
who had set himself to live only to serve. But had this
really been Don Quixote's sole aim ? We know already
that it was not so. In Don Quixote's idealism there had

been an element of Sancho even before Sancho had influenced him. Lofty as were his means, noble his ends, the hero in aiming at glory was aiming at something for himself. His selflessness was not complete. This element of egoism, spiritual as it was, was bound to chain him little by little to the material world, impoverishing his spirit until it became in essence on a level with that of his squire. And this equality, obscurely felt by Sancho, ends in destroying the respect he had at first for his master. So, in this scene of the Cave of Montesinos, we see Sancho twice contradicting his master flatly and insolently and Don Quixote answering with significant forbearance:

'But pardon me, good master of mine, I tell your worship, that, of all you have been saying, God take me (I was going to say the devil) if I believe one word.'

'How so?' said the scholar: 'Señor Don Quixote then must have lied; who, if he had a mind to it, has not had time to imagine and compose such a heap of lies.'

'I do not believe my master lies,' answered Sancho.

'If not, what do you believe?' quoth Don Quixote.

'I believe,' answered Sancho, 'that the same Merlin, or those necromancers, who enchanted all the crew your worship says you saw and conversed with there below, have crammed into your imagination or memory all this stuff you have already told us, or that remains to be told.'

'Such a thing might be, Sancho,' replied Don Quixote; 'but it is not so: for what I have related I saw with my own eyes, and touched with my own hands.'

'In an evil juncture, and in a worse season, and in a bitter day, dear patron of mine, did you go down to the other world; and in an unlucky moment did you meet with Señor Montesinos, who has returned you back to us in such guise. Your worship was very well here above, entirely in your senses, such as God had given you, speaking sentences, and giving advice at every turn, and not, as now, relating the greatest extravagances that can be imagined.'

'As I know you, Sancho,' answered Don Quixote, 'I make no account of your words.'

'Nor I of your worship's,' replied Sancho.

'O holy God!' cried Sancho aloud at this juncture, 'is it possible there should be such an one in the world, and that enchanters and enchantments should have such power over him, as to change my master's good understanding into so extravagant a madness? O sir! sir! for God's sake, look to yourself, and stand up for your honour, and give no credit to these vanities, which have diminished and decayed your senses.'

'It is your love of me, Sancho, makes you talk at this rate,' quoth Don Quixote.

Cervantes in the next chapter comments on the 'boldness of Sancho Panza' and the 'patience of his master', as well as 'the astonishment' which they struck into the cousin of the Knight of the Green Riding-coat who had witnessed them. But he limits himself to adding that the same cousin 'judged that the mildness of temper he [Don Quixote] then showed sprang from the satisfaction he had just received in seeing his mistress Dulcinea del Toboso, though enchanted'. The cousin 'judged' because he hardly knew the Knight and his squire. But Cervantes knew what the position was. The Knight has received his death-blow at the hands of his own ambition. In the adventure of Master Pedro, Sancho says to him:

'But for all that, . . . I should be glad your worship would desire Master Pedro to ask his ape, whether all be true, which befell you in the cave of Montesinos, because, for my own part, begging your worship's pardon, I take it to be all sham and lies, or at least a dream.'

'It may be so,' answered Don Quixote: 'but I will do

what you advise me, since I myself begin to have some kind of scruples about it.'

The sense of spiritual equality which this situation produces receives its final confirmation from the lips of Don Quixote himself at the end of the adventure of Clavileño:

'Sancho, since you would have us believe all you have seen in heaven, I expect you should believe what I saw in Montesinos' cave;—I say no more.'

The Rise of Sancho

WE have seen that, with the enchantment of Dulcinea, Cervantes initiates a new phase of his novel, in which his two protagonists move on levels not far apart. With Don Quixote depressed and humiliated, and Sancho strengthened and (in his own eyes) exalted, the relationship between the two has changed. It is no longer as before that of the Knight above over the squire below, but that of the influence now of Don Quixote on Sancho, now of Sancho on Don Quixote. In this phase the curves of the spiritual evolution of master and man are intertwined. But the general tendency is for Sancho to rise and Don Quixote to fall.

Vanity, self-importance, belief in himself grow apace in the Squire. When Don Quixote sends him on an embassy to offer his respects to the Duchess, he answers haughtily the counsels of prudence which his master gives him:

'You have hit upon the messiger,' quoth Sancho, 'why this to me? as if this were the first time I had carried a message to high and mighty ladies in my life.'

'Excepting that to the lady Dulcinea,' replied Don Quixote, 'I know of none you have carried, at least none for me.'

'That is true,' answered Sancho; 'but a good paymaster gives willing surety; and in the house of plenty, there is dinner for twenty: I mean, there is no need of advising me; for I am prepared for all, and have a smattering of everything.' (Part II, Chapter xxx.)

This belief in himself gives him the necessary assurance to cut in in conversations on a level with his betters. And so we see him telling the story of the

'Head of the Table' during lunch with the Duke and Duchess, advising them as to whether or not they should go out to receive the Countess Trifaldi: replying, before his master, to the afflicted Countess with an entertaining parody of her speech and interrupting the story with jests and gibes; speaking before his master, and in language imitated from him, when he saw the Countess faint, and finally letting his imagination run riot in the story of the seven goats apropos of the adventure of Clavileño.

Sancho's spirit is sustained on the one hand by the intimate conviction that he is the equal of his master in spirit; and on the other by the notion of his popularity as a personage in a printed history. We are reminded of this by Cervantes' frequent allusions to the printed history of Don Quixote. Thus, in the conversation with the Duchess, the vain squire says:

'So say I: that, if my lady Dulcinea del Toboso is enchanted, it is clear that I could not enchant her, but my master's enemies, who must needs be many and malicious: true it is, that she I saw was a country-wench: for such I took her, and such I judged her to be; and, if she was Dulcinea, it is not to be placed to my account, nor ought it to lie at my door, and to all that Good Bye! A fine thing, indeed, if I must be called in question at every turn, with, Sancho said it, Sancho did it, Sancho came back, and Sancho returned; as if Sancho were any one, and not that very Sancho Panza, handed about in print all the world over, as Sanson Carrasco told me, who is at least a bachelor of Salamanca; and such persons cannot lie, excepting when they have a mind to it, or when it turns to good account: so that there is no reason why anybody should fall upon me, since I have a good name; and, as I have heard my master say, a good name is better than great riches: case me but in this same government, and you will see wonders;

for a good squire will make a good governor.' (Part II, Chapter xxxiii.)

And when the Countess Trifaldi declares him indispensable to disenchant Antonomasia, Sancho reveals his new weakness, answering:

'In the king's name,' quoth Sancho, 'what have squires to do with their master's adventures? must they run away with the fame of those they accomplish, and must we undergo the fatigue? Body of me! did the historians but say, "Such a knight achieved such and such an adventure, with the help of such an one, his squire, without whom it had been impossible for him to finish it," it were something; but you shall have them dryly write thus: "Don Paralipomenon of the Three Stars, achieved the adventure of the six goblins"; without naming his squire, who was present all the while, as if there had been no such person in the world.' (Part II, Chapter xl.)

These, and other manifestations of the appetite for glory which has mastered Sancho, bring him so far as to seek to become a knight-errant, as he declares on his knees before the Duchess in language also imitated from his master:

'From great ladies great favours are to be expected: that which your ladyship has done me to-day, cannot be repaid with less than the desire of seeing myself dubbed a knight-errant, that I may employ all the days of my life in the service of so high a lady.'

On these heights Sancho passes through two trials, the paradoxical consequences of which reveal the wonderful psychological subtlety of Cervantes. From the summit of government Sancho comes out sobered and edified in his ambition. Through the humiliation of lashes and pinches he once more becomes vain and self-confident. The results of his experiment as governor are curious and complex. Sancho thought himself, there is no doubt of it, worthy to govern. The acumen, which like another Solomon he brought to the solving of problems with which he was faced, did not fail to have a good effect on himself, as well as on his observers. But that last adventure of the attack on the Island, along with the drubbing which the heartless servants of the Duke made him undergo, coming on top of the vexations and starvation the doctor Pedro Recio imposed on him, convince him that the governing of an island is not the soft and easy-going affair he had imagined. When this idea goes home to him Sancho reacts and realizes that, in desiring an island, he had not been well advised. This feeling of failure, this intimate humiliation, inspire that eloquent silence with which he makes his preparations for his unannounced departure, a scene of so clear an atmosphere and of such fine and true emotion :

He asked what o'clock it was; they told him it was daybreak. He held his peace; and, without saying anything more, he began to dress himself, buried in silence, and they all stared at him, in expectation what would be the issue of his dressing himself in such haste.

By this road of disillusionment Sancho reaches a philosophic state of mind which brings him to the renunciation of vain ambitions. With his arms round the neck of the donkey, witness of his simple past— his tranquil past—the erstwhile governor becomes once more a squire-errant. But not on this account does he renounce his individuality; quite the reverse. His self-esteem which we saw born and growing in him from the beginning of Part II, compromised momentarily by ambition, is saved by this act of wise renunciation and returns to seek its sustenance in experience. As in this life a man finds always what he seeks—if he knows how to look for it—Sancho found food for his vanity in the power to disenchant enchanted damsels, or raise others from the dead, which several more or less well-meaning sages detect in him. The conditions laid down by Merlin for disenchanting Dulcinea heighten his importance by making Don Quixote, in a certain degree, a slave to his good will. Sancho is not slow to feel this new importance added to that which he has already acquired. In the scene in which Merlin announces his new power to him and the enchanted Dulcinea throws at him a fairly virile string of insults for not agreeing to the sacrifice, Sancho replies with that speech, so true and entertaining in its incoherence and so significant of the importance which he attached to himself :

'Please, your grandeur, to let me alone,' answered Sancho; 'for at present I cannot stand to mind niceties, nor a letter more or less; for these lashes which are to be given me, or I must give myself, keep me so disturbed that I know not what I say, or what I do. But one thing I would fain know from the lady Dulcinea del Toboso, where she learned the way of entreaty she uses. She comes to desire me to tear my flesh with stripes, and at the same time calls me soul of a pitcher, and untamed beast; with such a bead-roll of ill names that the devil may bear them for me. What! does she think my flesh is made of brass? or is it anything to me whether she be disenchanted, or no? What basket of fine linen, shirts, night-caps, and socks (though I wear none), does she bring to mollify me, but reproach upon reproach, when she might have known the common proverb, that An Ass laden with gold mounts nimbly up the hill; and, Presents break rocks;

and, Pray to God devoutly, and hammer on stoutly; and, One take is worth two I'll give thee's? Then my master, instead of wheedling and coaxing me, to make myself of wool and carded cotton, says, if he takes me in hand, he will tie me naked with a rope to a tree, and double me the dose of stripes. Besides, these compassionate gentlefolks ought to consider, that they do not desire to have a squire whipped, but a governor, as one might say: Drink and with cherries. Let them learn, let them learn, I tell them, how to ask and entreat, and to have breeding; for all times are not alike, nor are men always in good humour. I am at this time just ready to burst with grief to see my green jacket torn; and people come to desire me to whip myself, of my own goodwill, I having as little mind to it as to become a cacique.' (Part II, Chapter xxxv).

Along this road, with the help of those who play on his credulity, Sancho gradually rises in his own esteem as a disenchanter of maidens. In his short second stay in the castle he saves Altisidora who had died of love, but comes to life again when Sancho allows himself to be pricked and pinched by the *dueñas*. This second adventure consecrates him in his own eyes as a disenchanter and a raiser from the dead. Thus commenting on the forgetfulness of Altisidora who, contrary to her promise, does not give him the six shirts, price of the sacrifice, the dejected squire says to his master:

'In truth, sir, I am the most unfortunate physician that is to be met with in the world, in which there are doctors, who kill the patient they have under cure, and yet are paid for their pains, which is no more than signing a little scroll of certain medicines, which the apothecary, not the doctor, makes up: while poor I, though another's cure cost me drops of blood, twitches, pinches, pin-prickings, and lashes, get not a doit. But I vow to God, if ever any sick body falls into my hands again, they shall grease them well before I perform the cure; for, The abbot must eat, that sings for his meat; and I cannot believe heaven has endued me with the virtue I have, that I should communicate it to others for nothing.'

And farther on, chatting in the Inn with Don Alvaro de Tarfe, the lucky mortal who succeeds in going down to posterity in the two second parts of the book—the real and the spurious—Sancho says with inimitable *naïveté* :

'Without doubt your worship must be enchanted, like my lady Dulcinea del Toboso : and would to heaven your disenchantment depended upon my giving myself another three thousand odd lashes, as I do for her; for I would lay them on, without interest or reward.'

The heroism of vanity cannot go farther.

The Decline of Don Quixote

THE end of the book is the slow and pathetic decline of the chivalrous spirit of the hero. In spite of the haste which drove his pen in the last stages of the work, written under the stimulus of the spurious *Quijote* of Avellaneda, Cervantes has measured in a masterly manner this gradual and inevitable decline, the key of which he gives at the beginning of his last chapter with that beautiful serenity, peculiarly his own: 'As all human things, especially the lives of men, are transitory, incessantly declining from their beginning till they arrive at their final end . . .'

Thus little by little we see Don Quixote's star pale. Once Dulcinea is enchanted, the Knight begins to lose that vital force of his which stood in place of serenity, and gave him strength to impose on himself and on others a reality created by his imagination. He no more takes inns for castles. He has been defeated and knows it. The attack on Master Pedro's puppets reveals the extent of the evil. Don Quixote, after the hallucination which led him to destroy the whole troop of puppets with a blow of his sword, gives explanations as spontaneous as they are humble and no less spontaneously offers to pay the damage:

'Now am I entirely convinced,' quoth Don Quixote, 'at this juncture, of what I have often believed before, that those enchanters who persecute me, are perpetually setting shapes before me as they really are, and, presently putting the change upon me, and transforming them into whatever they please. I protest to you, gentlemen that hear me, that whatever has passed at this time seemed to me to pass actually and precisely so: I took Melisendra to be Melisendra: Don Gayferos, Don Gayferos; Marsilio, Marsilio; and Charlemagne, Charlemagne. This it was that inflamed my choler; and, in compliance with the duty of my profession as a knight-errant, I had a mind to assist and succour those who fled; and with this good intention I did what you just now saw; if things have fallen out the reverse, it is no fault of mine, but of those my wicked persecutors; and notwithstanding this mistake of mine, and though it did not proceed from malice, yet will I condemn myself in costs. See, Master Pedro, what you must have for the damaged figures, and I will pay it you down in current and lawful money of Castile.'

Still more serious is the adventure of the braying aldermen. It will be remembered that this adventure seemed on the way to end with a mere homily of Don Quixote, when Sancho, with significant aplomb, decided not to be behind his master and to give a discourse also, which ended, very inopportunely, in a bray. Taken as a provocation by one of the sensitive inhabitants of the braying village, Sancho's peroration drew down the wrath of the villagers: Don Quixote tried to come to the aid of his squire:

. . . but so many interposed, that it was impossible for him to be revenged: on the contrary, finding a shower of stones come thick upon him, and a thousand cross-bows presented, and as many guns levelled at him, he turned Rocinante about, and, as fast as he could gallop, got out from among them, recommending himself to God with all his heart, to deliver him from this danger, fearing at every step, lest some bullet should enter at his back and come out at his breast; and at every moment he fetched his breath, to try whether it failed him or not. But those of the squadron were satisfied with seeing him fly, and did not shoot after him.

A curious episode and worthy of notice, as it presents us with a Don Quixote afraid, proof that our Knight's faith in himself, shaken by Sancho's triumph in the enchantment of Dulcinea, had sunk so low that it was not sufficient now to keep even his courage up.

With such ups and downs his faith lingers until his defeat by the Knight of the White Moon. Thus we see him set out on the adventure of the enchanted boat with a mettle which, at first, recalls his better days, but it soon spends itself in a discussion with the millers, and he falls into a typical discouragement of will:

Enough, thought Don Quixote to himself, it will be preaching in the desert, to endeavour, by entreaties, to prevail with such a mob to do anything that is honourable: and, in this adventure, two able enchanters must have engaged, the one frustrating what the other attempts, the one providing me a bark, and the other oversetting it: God help us! this world is nothing but machinations and tricks quite opposite one to the other: I can do no more. Then looking towards the mills, he raised his voice, and said: 'Friends, whoever you are that are enclosed in this prison, pardon me, that, through my misfortune and yours, I cannot deliver you from your affliction; this adventure is kept and reserved for some other knight.'

His arrival and stay in the house of the Duke and Duchess gives him some encouragement and confidence. But when Sancho remarks on the likeness between the Duke's steward and Countess Trifaldi, he has strength for no more than a cryptic answer ending in a request which seems almost a sign of fatigue:

'There is no need of the devil's running away with you, Sancho, either as an honest man, or a believer (for I know not what you mean). I see plainly the steward's face is the same with the Afflicted Lady's and yet the steward is not

the Afflicted Lady; for that would imply a palpable contra-
diction. But this is no time to enter into these inquiries,
which would involve us in an intricate labyrinth. Believe
me, friend, we ought earnestly to pray to our Lord, to
deliver us from wicked wizards and enchanters.'

Cervantes penetrates farther and farther into the
inner chambers of the mind of his hero, each more
obscure than the last, with that inimitable way of his—
perhaps not altogether conscious—that genius for
suggesting and for creating an atmosphere without
seeming to. The adventures of this last part of the book
all reveal a Don Quixote wearied to the innermost
springs of his being. When Doña Rodriguez comes
to beg the aid of his arm against the seducer of
her daughter, the Knight agrees unwillingly and with
words bordering on discourtesy :

To which words Don Quixote returned this answer,
with much gravity and solemnity : 'Good dueña, moderate
your tears, or rather dry them up, and spare your sighs;
for I take upon me the charge of seeing your daughter's
wrongs redressed; though it had been better if she had not
been so easy in believing the promises of lovers, who, for
the most part, are very ready in promising, and very slow
in performing.'

More characteristic if possible is his attitude in the
adventure of the holy images, in front of which he
pronounces these significant words :

'I take it for a good omen, brethren, to have seen what I
have seen : for these saints and knights professed what I
profess, which is, the exercise of arms : the only difference
between them and me is, that they were saints, and fought
after a heavenly manner, and I am a sinner, and fight after
an earthly manner. They conquered heaven by force of

arms (for heaven suffers violence), and I hitherto cannot tell what I conquer by force of my sufferings. But, could my Dulcinea del Toboso get out of hers, my condition being bettered, and my understanding directed aright, I might perhaps take a better course than I do.'

These words foreshadow the knight who is to contemplate passively the exploit of the brigand Roque Guinart.

But in this decline of Don Quixote there is a moment more pathetic than the rest, one which manifests and at the same time hastens it and which Cervantes has treated with special mastery. It is the period immediately following Sancho's rise to the governorship of the island of Barataria. Don Quixote's state of mind in regard to the unexpected realization of Sancho's dream is marvellously depicted. Two moods hold sway in him: sadness and a certain harshness due to offended pride, with a touch of shamefaced envy, a most complex state of mind revealing itself especially in the famous 'documents' or instructions which he gives Sancho. Cervantes emphasizes the sadness at the outset:

It is related then, that scarcely was Sancho departed, when Don Quixote felt his solitude and, had it been possible for him to have recalled the commission, and taken the government from him, he certainly would have done it.

The Duchess soon perceived his melancholy, and asked him why he was so sad: if for the absence of Sancho, there were squires, dueñas, and damsels enough in her house, ready to serve him to his heart's desire.

'It is true, madam,' answered Don Quixote, 'that I am concerned for Sancho's absence; but that is not the principal cause that makes me appear sad.'

and once brought to the surface this melancholy mood spreads and fills the whole atmosphere. On going to bed Don Quixote discovers one of his silk stockings in holes, whereupon Cervantes envelops his hero in an atmosphere of poverty which intensifies the melancholy. Whether by art or inadvertence, perhaps inadvertence and subconscious art, Cervantes puts his pathetic address to poverty in the mouth of Cide Hamete Ben Engeli, but ends saying: 'All these melancholy reflections recurred to Don Quixote's thoughts upon the rent in his stocking'; so that this melancholy discourse on poverty remains floating in the air like a kind of mist.

And it is well to point out here how in this culminating moment of the work, by a spiritual law (the one above influences the one below) the victorious Sancho influences the vanquished Don Quixote, and what the Knight feels, without being aware of it, is precisely the melancholy of poverty, the reverse side of the happiness of wealth, which is the ideal just attained by his successful squire.

The same influence is to be seen at work in the second feeling produced in Don Quixote by Sancho's rise. It comes out in a certain harshness, a certain aggressiveness in the tone he uses towards his servant, the brand-new governor:

'Infinite thanks give I to heaven, friend Sancho, that first, and before I have met with any good luck myself, good fortune has gone forth to meet and receive you. I, who had made over my future good success for the payment of your past services, find myself still at the beginning of my advancement, whilst you, before the due time, and against all rule of reasonable expectation, find yourself in full possession of your wishes. Others bribe, importune, solicit, attend early, pray, persist, and yet do not obtain what they aim at: another comes, and without knowing how or which way, carries that employment or office against all other pretenders. And this makes good the saying: in pretensions, luck is all. You, who in my opinion, are without doubt a blockhead, without rising early or sitting up late, and without taking any pains at all, by the air alone of knight-errantry breathing on you, see yourself, without more ado, governor of an island, as if it were a matter of nothing. All this I say, O Sancho, that you may not ascribe the favour done you to your own merit, but give thanks to heaven.' (Part II, Chapter xlii.)

The whole of this admirable page must be read between the lines for its wonderful psychological penetration, the intentions, motives, and passions that lurk under the words. Don Quixote appears in it impelled by a desperate desire to assert his superiority, reminding Sancho of his little wit, his small merits, and even his humble origin, not without provoking in the democratic Sancho a certain amount of serio-comic protest:

'Secondly, Consider who you were, and endeavour to know yourself, which is the most difficult point of knowledge imaginable. The knowledge of yourself will keep you from puffing yourself up, like the frog, who strove to equal herself to the ox; for the consideration of your having been a swineherd in your country will be, to the wheel of your fortune, like the peacock's ugly feet.'

'True,' answered Sancho; 'when I was a boy, I kept swine; but afterwards, when I grew towards man, I looked after geese, and not after hogs. But this, methinks, is nothing to the purpose; for all governors are not descended from the loins of kings.'

Much admiration has been wasted on Don Quixote's instructions, overlooking the fact that their only interest, even for Don Quixote, was as a means of raising himself above his successful inferior.

But even here the governing spirit of life which controls men takes its own way and these instructions themselves betray a Don Quixote strongly affected by the practical and positive sense of his squire. For, at the very moment when the Knight is trying to assert his moral superiority over Sancho, Cervantes has interspersed into both his attitude and his discourse clear proof of Sancho's influence over him, not only in the matter of some of the instructions given, but even in the language and in the attitude of Don Quixote towards the wealth of proverbs which Sancho was wont to use.

Don Quixote's subconscious tendency to imitate Sancho's language has appeared already in preceding chapters. The clearest instance is perhaps at the end of Don Quixote's speech at dessert with the Duke and Duchess. Cervantes, with his usual insight, puts this imitation of Sancho's style into Don Quixote's mouth at the moment when Don Quixote is speaking precisely of his squire. The imitation cannot be more patent:

'In short I would not exchange him for any other squire, though a city were given me to boot: and therefore I am in doubt, whether I shall do well to send him to the government your grandeur has favoured him with: though I perceive in him such a fitness for the business of governing, that, with a little polishing of his understanding, he would be as much master of that art, as the king is of his customs. Besides, we know by sundry experiences, that there is no need of much ability, nor much learning, to be a governor; for there are a hundred of them up and

down that can scarcely read, and yet they govern as sharp
as so many hawks. The main point is, that their intention
be good, and that they desire to do everything right, and
there will never be wanting counsellors to advise and
direct them in what they are to do; like your governors,
who being swordsmen, and not scholars, have an assistant
on the bench. My counsel to him would be : All bribes to
refuse, but insist on his dues; with some other little
matters, which lie in my breast, and shall out in proper
time, for Sancho's benefit, and the good of the island he is
to govern.'

This passage must be put alongside of the ones we
have already mentioned in which Sancho, speaking to
Teresa Panza, makes a comic use of language inspired
by that of his master.

In this subtle, quiet, and indirect way, Cervantes
suggests the growing influence of Sancho on Don
Quixote, which comes so plainly to the surface in the
scene of the instructions. Here Don Quixote again
reprehends Sancho's mania for proverbs, but this time
reveals plainly what now and then on previous occasions we have adumbrated : his irritation at this feature
in the style of his squire. Among his instructions Don
Quixote aims at Sancho a somewhat venomous one :

'Likewise, Sancho, intermix not in your discourse that
multitude of proverbs you are wont : for, though proverbs
are short judgements, you often drag them in so by the
head and shoulders, that they seem rather nonsense than
judgements.'

And on Sancho's replying with a long string of them,
Don Quixote answers him :

'Go on, Sancho, Go on,' quoth Don Quixote, 'thrust in,
heap up, string on your proverbs, for nobody can beat
you. My mother whips me, and I tear on. I am warning

you to abstain from proverbs, and in an instant you pour forth a litany of them, which square with what we are upon as much as, Over the hills and far away. Look you, Sancho, I do not say a proverb is amiss when skilfully applied; but to accumulate, and string them at random, renders a discourse flat and low.'

In which a good deal of his adversary's ammunition is to be found. Not long after Don Quixote surrenders and lets out his inmost thought:

'Oh! God's curse light on you,' cried out Don Quixote at this instant, 'sixty thousand devils take you, and your proverbs! You have been stringing of them this full hour, and putting me to the rack with every one of them. Take my word for it, these proverbs will one day bring you to the gallows: upon their account, your subjects will strip you of your government, or at least conspire against you. Tell me, where find you them, ignorant? or how apply you them, dunce? For my own part, to utter but one, and apply it properly, I sweat and labour as if I were digging.'

A revelation of secret envy, a humble capitulation which the discouraged Knight is to carry still farther. On Sancho answering:

'Before God, master of mine . . . your worship complains of very trifles. Why the devil are you angry, that I make use of my own goods? for I have no other, nor any stock, but proverbs upon proverbs: and just now I have four that present themselves pat to the purpose, and sit like pears in a pannier; but I will not produce them: for, To keep silence well is called Sancho.'

Don Quixote says between pride and defeat:

'That Sancho is not you; for not only you are not keeping silence well, but you are speaking ill and ever discussing. But, for all that, I would fain know what four proverbs occurred to you just now, so pat to the purpose;

for I have been running over my own memory, which is a pretty good one, and I can think of none.'

So down the narrow and stony road leading from pride to humiliation the unfortunate Knight proceeds, revealing to us the decline of his spirit alongside the rise of that of Sancho.

Farther on, Chapter lxvii, Part II, we shall hear him again correcting Sancho in Sancho's own style:

'No more proverbs, good Sancho,' quoth Don Quixote; 'for any one of those you have mentioned is sufficient to let us know your meaning. I have often advised you not to be so prodigal of your proverbs, and to keep a strict hand over them: but, it seems, it is preaching in the desert, and, The more my mother whips me, the more I rend and tear.'

calling forth a deserved criticism from Sancho:

'Methinks,' answered Sancho, 'your worship makes good the saying, The kettle called the pot black-eyed. You are reproving me for speaking proverbs, and you string them yourself by couples.'

Cervantes gives a sense of complete inversion of styles in which each of the characters observes the effects of his own influence on the other, without realizing the cause. (Part II, Chapter lxviii.)

'I know not what that means,' replied Sancho: 'I only know, that while I am asleep, I have neither fear nor hope, neither trouble nor glory; and, blessings on him who invented sleep, the mantle that covers all human thoughts, the food that appeases hunger, the drink that quenches thirst, the fire that warms cold, the cold that moderates heat, and, lastly, the general coin that purchases all things, the balance and weight that equals the shepherd with the king, and the simple with the wise. One only evil, as I have heard, sleep has in it, namely, that it resembles death; for between a man asleep and a man dead, there is but little difference.'

'I never heard you, Sancho,' quoth Don Quixote, 'talk so elegantly as now; whence I come to know the truth of the proverb you often apply, Not with whom thou art bred, but with whom thou art fed.'

'Dear master of mine,' replied Sancho, 'it is not I that am stringing of proverbs now; for they fall from your worship's mouth also by couples, faster than from me; only between yours and mine there is this difference, that your worship's come at the proper season, and mine out of season; but, in short, they are all proverbs.'

Cervantes prepares us in this way for the final defeat of his hero. The manner and detail of this defeat are of no special importance. He was beaten, and from that moment deemed himself unworthy of life and abandoned himself to his sad destiny. The author multiplies on the return journey the situations in which Sancho is seen full of spirit and Don Quixote without faith. When asked for advice about a race by some peasants:

'Not so,' quoth Sancho immediately, before Don Quixote could answer: 'and to me, who have so lately left being a governor and a judge, as all the world knows, it belongs to resolve these doubts, and give my opinion in every controversy.'

'Answer in a good hour, friend Sancho,' quoth Don Quixote; 'for I am not fit to feed a cat, my brain is so disturbed and turned topsy-turvy.'

In the adventure of the pigs:

Sancho got up as well as he could, and desired his master to lend him his sword, saying, he would kill half a dozen of those unmannerly gentlemen swine, for such by this time he knew them to be.

Said Don Quixote to him: 'Let them alone, friend; for this affront is a punishment for my sin; and it is a just judgement of heaven, that wild dogs should devour, wasps sting, and hogs trample upon, a vanquished knight-errant.'

And thus the Knight of the Sorrowful Figure returns to his village, no longer leading Sancho but led by him. When at the end of the journey 'they ascended a little hill, from whence they discovered their village', it is Sancho who feels in his heart the lyrical impulse of victory. He carries back wealth. He has been a governor. He has the power to disenchant and bring back to life young maidens. His is famous. And so the good squire falls on his knees and says:

'Open thine eyes, O desired country, and behold thy son Sancho Panza, returning to thee again, if not very rich, yet very well whipped! Open thine arms, and receive likewise thy son Don Quixote, who, if he comes conquered by another's hand, yet he comes a conqueror of himself, which, as I have heard him say, is the greatest victory that can be desired! Money I have; for, if I was well whipped, I rode at ease.'

and it is Don Quixote who cuts him short, saying drily: 'Leave those fooleries.'

So, when on his death-bed, having gained his reason and lost his reasons for living, his friends try to raise his spirits reminding him of his past delusion, the Knight answers with a proverb, graceful and poetical as befits Don Quixote, yet drawn from Sancho's sack of truths, a proverb which unites the two men as brothers in a final embrace: 'There are no birds this year in the nests of yesteryear.'